“I really enjoyed readi
It has a lot of insight t
and levels of play impı
—D

former Major League player

“Mike Eden was a natural hitter and a tough man to get out. The techniques he used as a hitter will help every baseball player perform at a higher level. This book is great!”

—**Larry Doby Johnson**, *youth instructor,*
former Major League player

“As a college player, Mike was one of the best hitters to ever play for me. His book is filled with good, sound hitting fundamentals—it also teaches players confidence and mental proficiency!”

—**Richard “Itchy” Jones**, *former*
professional player, college
baseball coach for 35 years

“From bunting to hitting with the count and game situation hitting, this book covers all you need to know about being the best hitter you can be.

“I would especially recommend this book to young hitters—*before* they develop bad habits. It is also a good reference book for coaches—these hitting principles will help coaches teach young hitters good baseball.”

—**Wayne Tyrone**, *youth instructor,*
former Major League player

“Excellent book on hitting—baseball techniques that I have used throughout my career! We use many of these same principles in teaching at the Hitting Zone!”

—**David Kent**, *former professional player,*
youth instructor for 29 years

BE THE BEST BASEBALL HITTER YOU CAN BE

by
Edward Michael Eden

Edited by
Kirt M. Dressler

Chicago Spectrum Press
4824 Brownsboro Center
Louisville, Kentucky 40207
502-899-1919

Printed in the U.S.A.

10 9 8 7 6 5 4 3 2 1

ISBN: 1-58374-038-4

To order more copies of this book–
Email: mikeedenbaseball
or write:
Mike Eden
PO Box 280328, Tampa, FL 33682
$14.95 plus $4 shipping and handling,
$2.00 each additional book
(Florida residents please add $1.05 state tax)
Make checks payable to Mike Eden

ACKNOWLEDGMENTS

Special thanks to my good friend Kevin Fimbel, whose computer skills helped make this book possible.

Special thanks to my son, Matthew, for his great effort and patience throughout the many picture taking sessions.

CONTENTS

INTRODUCTION

I fell in love with baseball as a kid, and I still love it. I played baseball for 25 years, 9 years professionally. In 7 of those 9 professional years, I played year-round. I also player/coached, player/managed, and managed at the professional level.

While I did not get as much playing time as I would have liked in the Majors, I am still very proud of the career I had. I batted over .300 in all 5 professional seasons that I was a starter, and I enjoyed many other hitting accomplishments—both as an amateur and as a professional.

After being out of baseball for a number of years, I placed my 6-year-old son in T-ball. During the next several years, volunteers would often teach my son baseball one way, while I was teaching him another. I decided that it would be a good idea to write a book—one that would provide volunteers with professional baseball knowledge.

I wanted a book that would explain and illustrate the very best hitting fundamentals. My book should also explain how to *mentally* approach hitting. To be the best player you can be, studying the mental aspects of baseball is a must.

I had a specific goal of creating a book that was totally original. This was an easy goal to accomplish because I had not read any baseball books since childhood. Many of my friends suggested that I go to book stores and look at other baseball books, but I was determined to be original. With my 25 years of experience in baseball, I felt that I had all the knowledge necessary to produce the best book ever on hitting.

My *ultimate* goal, however, was to write a book on hitting that would be of great value to *all* baseball people. *Be the Best Baseball Hitter You Can Be* is designed to help not only young baseball players, but also Major Leaguers, managers, coaches, girls in softball, and adult softball players. (Although softball pitches are different, the hitting principles are the same.) *Be the Best Baseball Hitter You Can Be* is especially valuable to teenage players who are serious about making it to the top. It is a book they can read, study, and put into practice themselves.

My baseball coach at Southern Illinois University, Richard "Itchy" Jones, used to talk to us about hustling, working hard, and giving it all we had. He would tell us, "Don't look back years from now and wonder how good you could have been if you had only tried harder, because you have that chance right now!"

Not everyone has the ability and determination necessary to reach the Major Leagues, but becoming a better hitter will make your baseball experience a more fun and satisfying one.

1

BAT SELECTION

Select a Bat You Can Handle. *You must be able to swing quickly.* A heavier bat provides greater force when you hit the ball, but only if you can get it around in time. The great Ted Williams used a light bat, and slugger Jack Clark used a short 32-inch bat. Other great hitters like Dick Allen and Mike Piazza have used bigger and heavier bats quite successfully. Find the length and weight that you can handle.

Wood Bats. When selecting a wood bat, look for wide grain wood. Wide grain means there is a sizable area of solid wood between the softer age lines. If the lines on the hitting surface of your bat are at least 1/8 of an inch apart, you have a very solid bat (figs. 1 & 2). Thin grain wood is lighter, but it is also softer and more likely to dent or split apart.

Thin grain.
fig. 1

Wide grain.
fig. 2

2

GRIP

Cocking Your Wrists. When gripping the bat—cock your wrists *inward,* but not to the point of feeling awkward (fig. 3).

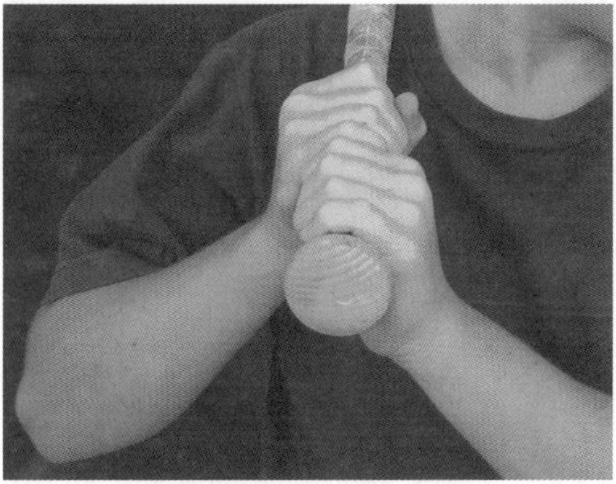

Wrists cocked inward.
fig. 3

The more your wrists are cocked, the faster they roll over. The faster they roll over, the more speed your bat has. This is called having good **"wrist action."** The result is a more powerful swing. Although Houston Astros left fielder Jimmy Wynn weighed only 165 pounds, he was a feared home run hitter because of his great wrist action.

Lining up Your Knuckles. Lining up your knuckles will ensure that your wrists are well cocked. Be sure to line up the knuckles as pictured (fig. 4). If you have trouble lining up these knuckles perfectly, *just come close and your results will still be great.*

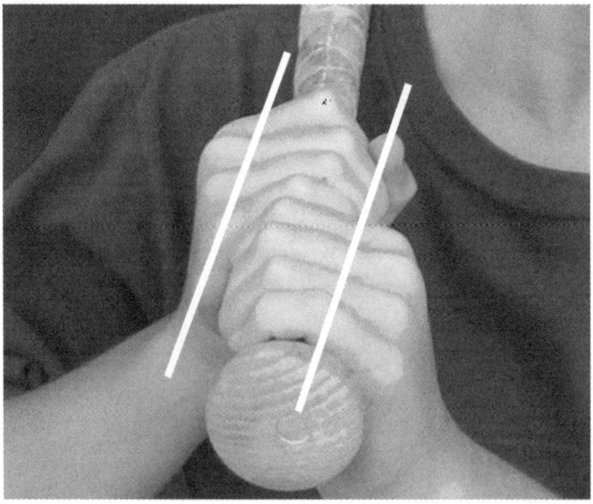

Lining up the knuckles.
fig. 4

Fingers. Angle your fingers slightly (fig. 5). This makes lining up the knuckles easier and cocking the wrists more comfortable. It also enables your fingers to provide more bat control and your back elbow to maintain correct positioning.

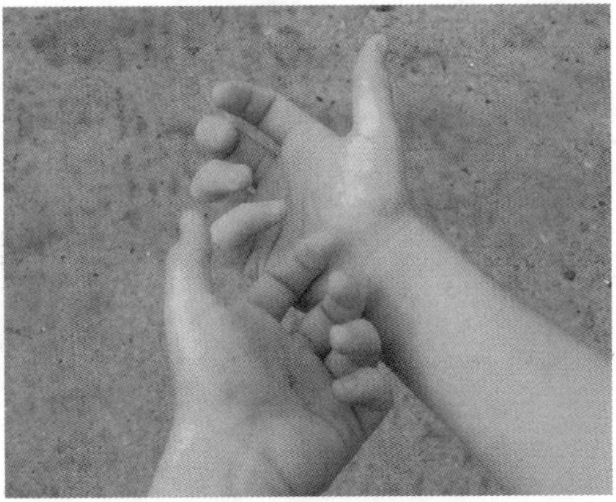

Angle the fingers slightly.
fig. 5

3

PLACEMENT IN THE BATTER'S BOX

Now you are ready to take your place in the batter's box. Step up to the plate and **stand in the back of the box** (fig. 6). This creates more distance between you and the pitcher, giving you another split second to see the pitch. Now you have more time to recognize the pitch and decide whether to swing or not.

Many coaches tell young players to move up in the box and get the curveball before it breaks. This is bad advice. You must learn how to *adjust* to pitches of different speeds and movements.

Moving up in the box puts you closer to the pitcher and prevents you from getting "a good look at the pitch"—one of the most essential parts of hitting. And what will you do if the pitch is an inside fastball and *not* a curve or change-up?

Look at Major League hitters, and you will see that none of them stand in the front of the box.

Make sure you can reach any part of the plate with the good part of your bat (fig. 7).

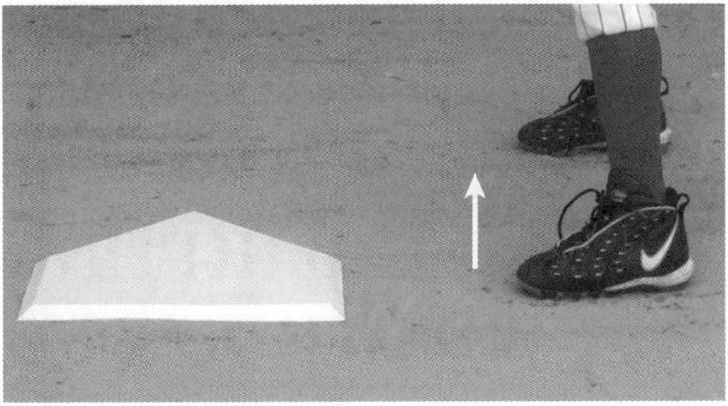

Stand back in the box.
fig. 6

Reach any part of the plate.
fig. 7

4

STANCE AND HITTING POSITION

Stance Variations

Your stance is the position of your entire body in the batter's box, ready for the pitch.

There are 3 main ways to describe batting stances.

1) How the front of the body is positioned to the pitcher
2) How a player stands
3) How a player holds the bat

How the Body is Positioned. A stance can be: ***closed***—body "turned away" from the pitcher (fig. 8), ***open***—body "facing" the pitcher (fig. 9), or ***straight***—body sideways to the pitcher (fig 10).

How a Player Stands. Players can assume a *straight-up* stance, or they can bend the knees and lean over in a *crouched* stance. Stances are described by how much a player stands straight-up or crouched.

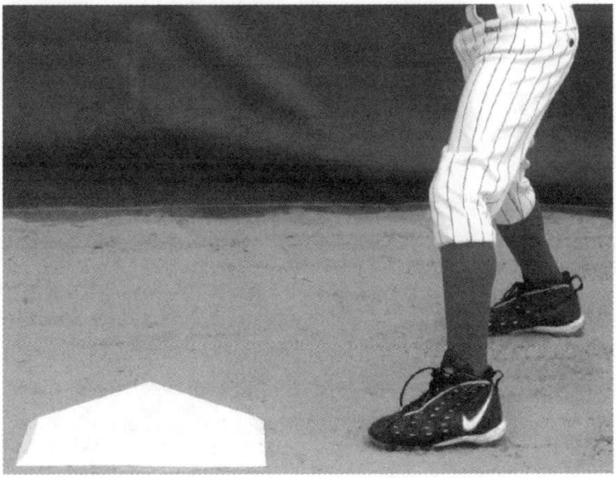

Closed stance.
fig. 8

Open stance.
fig. 9

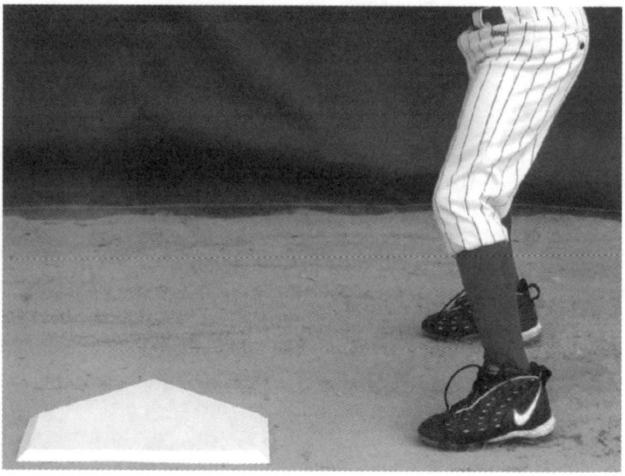

Straight Stance.
fig. 10

How a Player Holds the Bat. Players can hold the bat in many possible positions (fig. 11). *However, no matter what their style, at some point in the swing all hitters must arrive at the "hitting position." So why not start there?*

The Hitting Position

- To locate the *hitting position*, grip your bat and rest it on your back shoulder at a 45 degree angle. Then bring your hands out and back a little (fig. 12).

  Most Major League hitters place their hands in or near the *hitting position* when they assume their stance. Some bring their hands to the hitting position just before they swing. A few great hitters—like Sammy Sosa and Juan Gonzalez—are able to hold the bat in very different positions from the majority of players and still achieve good results.

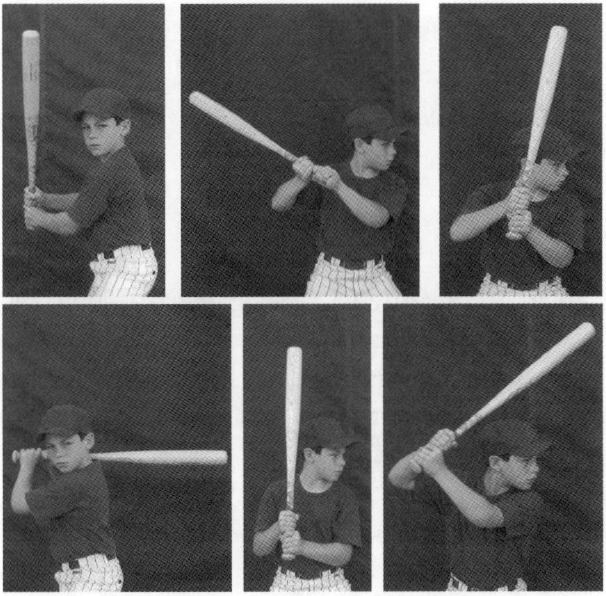

A few of the many possible positions the bat can be held in.
fig. 11

Hands in the hitting position.
fig. 12

Hitting Goals. Use a hitting style that gives you:

1) A good look at the pitch
2) Quickness
3) Speed
4) Power

A good look at the pitch is seeing the ball long enough to recognize what the pitch is. **Quickness** is getting your swing to the ball as soon as possible. **Speed** is how fast your bat moves during your swing. **Power** is the force you hit the ball with.

The fundamentals and techniques in this book are designed to promote the accomplishment of these hitting goals.

Taking Your Full Stance

You know where to stand in the box. You have the correct grip. Your hands are in the hitting position. Now let's position the rest of your body.

- **Feet.** Your back foot should point perpendicular to the side of the plate, while your front foot is angled slightly towards the playing field (fig. 13). Place your feet as they are pictured, relative to the plate.

- **Every Player is Different.** You must realize that because of size, shape, and strength, you may not be at your best trying to hit like your favorite player. You must bat the way *you* hit best.

- **Straight, Open, or Closed.** The **straight stance** gives you a good view of the pitcher and places the body in a good hitting position. The **open stance** provides an even better view and is more comfortable, but you must move back to the plate to swing. Many hitters prefer the **closed stance**, because it helps promote a powerful swing.

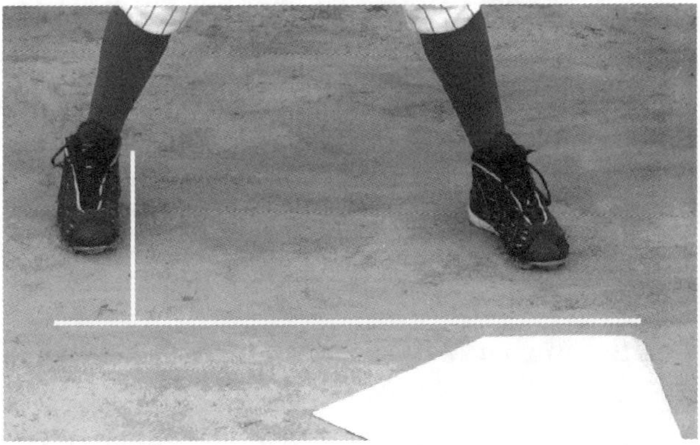

Placement of feet in the box.
fig. 13

A slightly closed stance of a few inches positions you for power, and you still have a good view of the pitcher. Mike Piazza, slugger for the New York Mets, uses a slightly closed stance. (He also places his hands in the hitting position.) Mike is a lifetime .325 hitter.

Try these stances in practice and see which style works best for *you*.

- **Knees.** Slightly bending the knees promotes quickness. Think of starting to run. You cannot go anywhere until you bend your knees. Bending the knees also means a better bat angle at the low strike.

Some hitters have experienced success using a straight-up stance. Dodgers first baseman Steve Garvey and Angels slugger Don Baylor are examples of this. However, most hitters prefer to bend the knees.

- **Leaning Over.** When the knees are bent, leaning over towards the plate helps promote balance and quickness. It also levels your bat angle a little at the low strike and brings your eyes closer to the pitch. Some hitters wait until the pitcher releases the ball to lean over, which saves wear and tear on the back. St. Louis Cardinals outfielder Jim Edmonds uses this technique.

- **Positioning Your Bat.** Point your bat straight back or tilt the top end slightly towards the pitcher. A forward tilt of a few inches places your bat in a great position for quickness and power (fig. 12).

  Use the 45 degree front angle rather than straight-up-and-down or parallel to the ground (fig. 14). If you do not like this angle, at least try to stay within a 35-50 degree range.

Good bat angle, 45 degrees.
fig. 14

Many hitters hold the bat upright, flat, or in other positions, then move to the 45 degree angle just before they swing. A's/Cardinals slugger Mark McGwire used this approach.

- **Positioning the Shoulders and Elbows.** When placing your shoulders and elbows in position, think of distance from the ground. Your front shoulder, the one closest to the pitcher, should be lower than the back shoulder. Your front elbow should be lower than your back elbow. This places your arms and shoulders in a cocked position, enabling you to swing with more power.

Your front elbow should be fairly close to your body now, with your back elbow up higher and pointing at the catcher's head.

Many coaches yell about getting the back elbow up high, even to the point of positioning it over your head and aiming it at the sky. Please, do not listen to this. However, never forget that it should be higher than the front elbow.

You are now in the best possible hitting stance to accomplish the 4 hitting goals listed earlier—getting a good look at the pitch, quickness, speed, and power (fig. 15).

Best hitting stance.
fig. 15

5

PREPARING FOR THE PITCH

Before taking your swing, you must **"prepare for the pitch."** When you are in your stance and waiting for the pitcher to throw the ball, *you must not stay* **"frozen"** *in one position too long without moving.* If you do, it can affect your sense of timing and cause you to swing a little too soon or a little too late. In order to prevent this from happening, you must have a means of staying *prepared for the pitch.*

There are a number of methods used by Major League hitters to *prepare for the pitch.* The best method is the one that works best for each individual hitter. The 7 most popular choices are illustrated on the following pages. Try these methods and see which one works best for *you.*

1) Take your stance and **"waggle" the bat** down low. That is, move it back and forth by rolling your wrists. Bring your bat up and into the hitting position as the pitcher takes his windup or stretch (fig. 16).

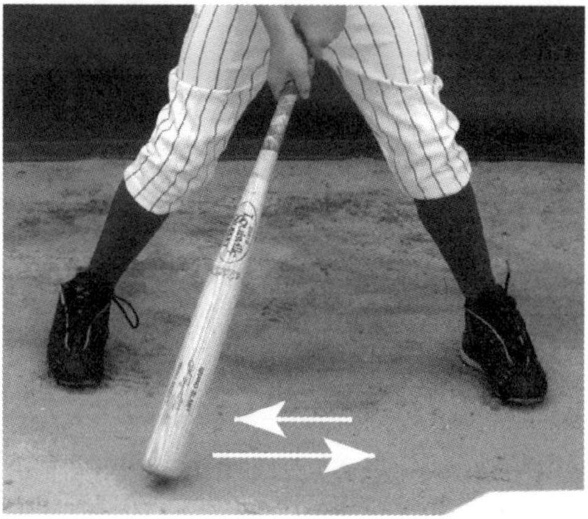

The "waggle."
fig. 16

Used by: Cardinals first baseman, **Mark McGwire**. In 1998, Mark hit 70 home runs, breaking Roger Maris' single season record of 61. McGwire later changed his style and did not roll the wrists in a waggle, but he still moved the bat down low for his preparation.

Rockies first baseman, **Todd Helton**. .336 average, 54 doubles, 49 home runs, 146 RBI in 2001.

2) Or, **take short practice swings**. Start an easy swing—but stop short of your follow-through. Repeat this short practice swing as needed until the pitcher takes his windup or stretch (fig. 17).

The short practice swing.
fig. 17

Used by: Cubs/Diamondbacks first baseman, **Mark Grace**. Mark had more hits than any other player in the 1990s.

Astros second baseman, **Craig Biggio**. 51 doubles in 1998, 56 doubles in 1999.

3) Another successful method is to swing or waggle the bat a few times, then **stand with your bat relaxed**. As the pitcher releases the ball, raise your bat and move into your stance (figs. 18a & b).

Bat relaxed.
fig. 18a

Bat ready.
fig. 18b

Used by: Astros left fielder, **Lance Berkman**. Lance keeps his bat relaxed (left-handed) until it is time to swing. .331 average, 55 doubles, 34 home runs, 126 RBI in 2001.

Angels outfielder, **Darin Erstad**. Darin began using this method in 2001. (See page 24 for some of his 2000 stats.)

4) Some hitters swing or waggle, then **hold the bat out front** until the pitcher takes his windup or stretch. Then they move into their stance (fig. 19).

Holding the bat out front.
fig. 19

Used by: Indians first baseman, **Jim Thome**. 37 home runs, 106 RBI in 2000. 49 home runs, 124 RBI in 2001.

A's/Devil Rays outfielder, **Ben Grieve**. 27 home runs, 104 RBI in 2000.

5) Many hitters like to **move the bat (or the hands and the bat) in a circular motion** (fig. 20).

Circular bat movement.
fig. 20

Used by: Red Sox/Devil Rays, **Wade Boggs**. 3,000+ hits, 5-time batting champ, career .328 average.

Reds center fielder, **Ken Griffey, Jr.** 40 home runs, 118 RBI in 2000. 460 homers through 2001.

6) Others like to **move the bat in a forward-and-back motion** (fig. 21).

Forward-and-back bat movement.
fig. 21

Used by: Giants left fielder, **Barry Bonds**. 49 home runs, 106 RBI in 2000. In 2001, Barry hit 73 home runs, breaking Mark McGwire's single season record of 70. He also batted .328 and drove in 137 runs.

Dodgers outfielder, **Gary Sheffield**. .325 average, 43 home runs, 109 RBI in 2000. 36 home runs, 100 RBI in 2001.

7) You can also **move the bat in an up-and-down motion** (fig. 22).

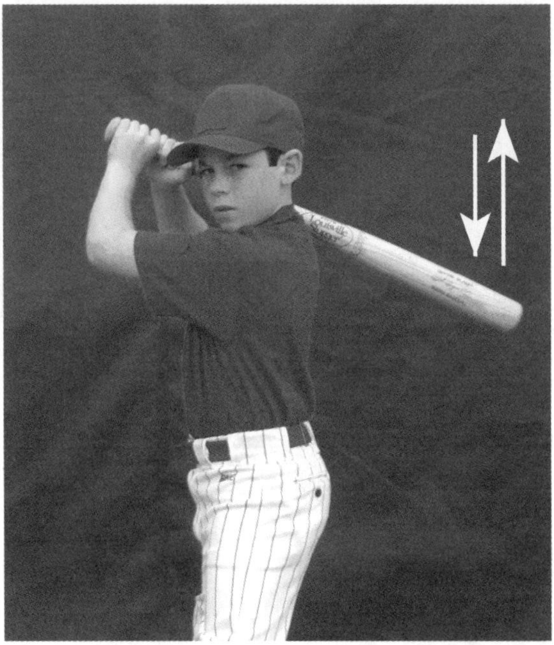

Up-and-down bat movement.
fig. 22

Used by: Diamondbacks outfielder, **Luis Gonzalez**. .325 average, 57 home runs, 142 RBI in 2001. Luis steadies his bat in the hitting position just before it is time to swing.

Angels outfielder, **Darin Erstad**. .355 average, 240 hits, 100 RBI in 2000.

Mariners second baseman, **Bret Boone**. 37 home runs, 141 RBI in 2001.

6

THE SWING

Every great hitter has a great swing. ***You* can have a great swing by developing good fundamentals and by hitting the ball with the most effective swing angle.** Although the *swing angle* is not often discussed, *it is a defining technique*!

Swing Angle

I have seen many Little League coaches teach young players to swing down at the ball. The Houston Astros even taught swinging down in the late 1960s. But tune in any Major League game and you will rarely see a hitter swing down at the ball. In fact, I know of only one or two Major League players who do (although there could be more). *Almost every player hits the ball with a slight uppercut.*

A slight uppercut of 0-3 degrees is good—3-6 degrees is great—6 degrees is super. Some players, like Ken Griffey, Jr. and Jim Edmonds, are often up around 10 or 20 degrees and even higher. However, the more you uppercut, the more precise and stronger you must be.

Once you master good fundamentals, hitting the ball with a 6 degree uppercut gives you the "Major League Swing." It is simply the angle the world's best hitters use when putting the bat on the ball (fig. 23).

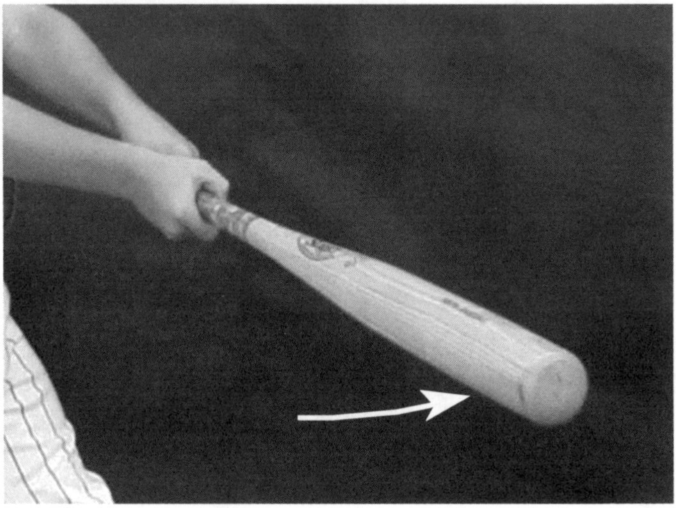

The Major League Swing, angle of 6 degrees.
fig. 23

Think about it. Swinging down produces a lot of ground balls. Do you want to be the hardest singles hitter on the planet, or would you like to hit the ball to the fence and beyond? I have seen 75 lb. kids in Little League use a good swing and hit with more power than much bigger kids who chop down at the ball.

If you are not using the 6 degree swing angle, it is time to start. You will get more extra base hits, and that will make you a more productive hitter.

Be sure not to swing up *too much*. Swinging up too much is just as bad as chopping down at the ball (this will soon be discussed).

Fundamentals of the Swing

You develop great technique by starting off with good fundamentals. Fundamentals are basic moves. Practice good fundamentals until you are skilled at them. Then put your skilled fundamentals all together and you have great technique. The way you use your technique is your style.

As you learn the fundamentals of the swing, think of how they work together to make up the total swing.

Now imagine you are up to bat. The pitcher is on the rubber and ready. You are at the plate and prepared for the pitch.

- **Body Weight in Your Stance.** Stand with about 60% of your weight on your back foot and 40% on your front foot.

- **Seeing the Ball.** Concentrate on visually "picking up" the ball as it comes out of the pitcher's hand. Pitchers have different release points, and you must see the ball as soon as possible.

- **Dragging the Bat.** A common hitting mistake some young players make is to "drag" the bat slowly forward before it is time to swing. Although your hands are bringing the bat forward, the swing has not begun. This makes the swing smaller and takes away your power. Instead, prepare yourself *mentally* to stride and swing—*concentrate on keeping your hands back until you have made the decision to swing.* Once you have made that decision, move forward quickly.

  Stride. Take a short stride of 6 inches or less. If you use a wide stance, do not stride more than a couple of inches.

The shorter your stride, the longer you can wait on the ball because your swing is quicker. As a result, you get a better look at the pitch.

Right-handed batters—point your front foot at the second baseman when you stride. *Left-handed batters*—point your front foot at the shortstop when you stride. This allows your body to turn more.

Keep your weight on the ball of your back foot and be sure to turn the back foot inwards. This turns your back knee and your hips, giving you a more complete and powerful swing. When you make contact with the ball, your back foot should point towards the pitcher (fig. 24).

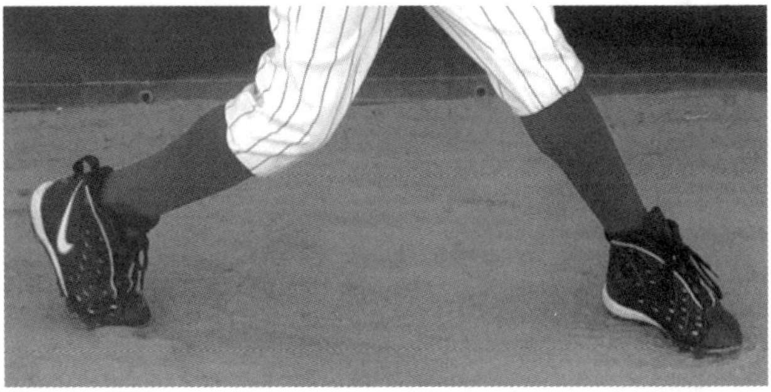

Pointing the front foot out, turning the back foot in.
fig. 24

This footwork is extremely important. It is almost impossible to turn your body and take a full swing without doing these things because your feet, knees, and hips remain locked. Matt Williams and Greg Vaughn are the only players I have ever seen swing without turning the back foot. They are both great hitters, but I do not know how they do it. It hurts my knees just to watch them.

Please note that when hitting a pitch on the outside corner, you will turn your back foot and body to a lesser degree. That pitch should be hit to the opposite field and, when hitting to the opposite field, your body should face that way more.

For right-handed batters, right field is the opposite field, center field is "up the middle," and left field is pulling the ball. For left-handed batters, it is the reverse.

- **The "V".** There is a hitting method going around called swinging with the "V" motion. People who promote this swing want you to chop down and then come back up immediately—like a V. Think about this. If you are just a little bit late with your swing, you will be chopping down at the ball. If you are too early, you will be swinging up at the ball too much. The V motion provides only 1 point and little time for good contact.

- **The "U".** The motion of your hands should be more like a "U" (fig. 25). When you swing with the U motion, you have more area and time for good contact. As a result, it is much easier to hit the ball with the desired 6 degree swing angle.

- **Swinging Up.** While swinging down at the ball does not produce desired results, swinging up too much is just as bad. If you are not extremely strong and talented, anything more than 6 degrees is too much.

When a hitter is swinging up too much and popping out, many coaches will shout, "You're dropping your back shoulder." This has always been the accepted reason for swinging up. However, this is not the real problem.

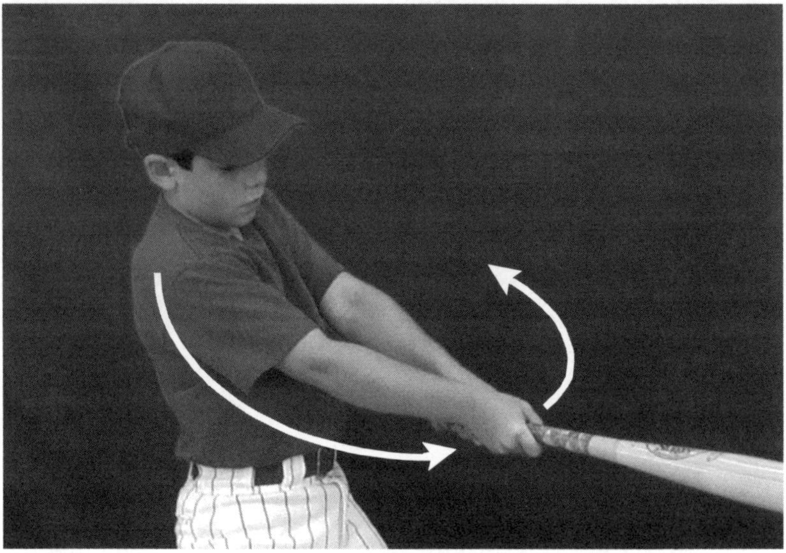

The "U."
fig. 25

Your back shoulder and elbow drop naturally as the swing unfolds. *The problem occurs when the top hand drops below the lead hand too much.* When this happens, the bat head falls down below the hands more than it should, forcing you to uppercut.

Look at your bat when your top hand is in its correct position (fig. 26a). Now look at your bat at the same point in time when your top hand has dropped too much (fig. 26b). The bat head is too low, and it is also late in coming around.

Pulling up the front elbow and shoulder too much can be a part of the problem, so concentrate on using the correct swing angle and do not think about "lifting" the ball out of the park—think about driving it out.

Top hand correct.
fig. 26a

Top hand too low.
fig. 26b

Dropping your hands from the hitting position can also cause you to swing up too much (and to miss). If you do not bring your hands back up before swinging, you will have trouble maintaining a good swing. The more you drop your hands, and the higher the pitch, the more trouble you will have.

As your hands move from the hitting position to the point of contact, your top hand should level out and finish just a little bit lower than the lead hand on high strikes—on middle strikes, it should finish a little lower still. On low strikes, the top hand must finish a good deal lower than the lead hand (in order to reach those pitches).

- **Overswinging.** Overswinging is trying to hit the ball harder than you really can. Most hitters experience this problem at some point in time. Overswinging causes breakdowns in your hitting fundamentals, such as overstriding and taking your eye off the ball. The end result of overswinging is fewer base hits. Hit the ball as hard as you can—but do not overswing.

- **Timing.** Now let's focus on perhaps the most important aspect of hitting: timing.

  Were you ever surprised by taking what you thought was just an easy swing and hitting the ball a long, long way? You hardly felt it. You hit it on the "good" part of the bat, but you also had great timing.

  Perfect timing is hitting the ball at your precise moment of maximum power.

When you swing the bat, speed helps produce power. **The greatest speed your bat reaches is when you are right in the middle of rolling your wrists over.** This is when your top hand is directly over your lead hand (fig. 27). This is when you want to meet the ball.

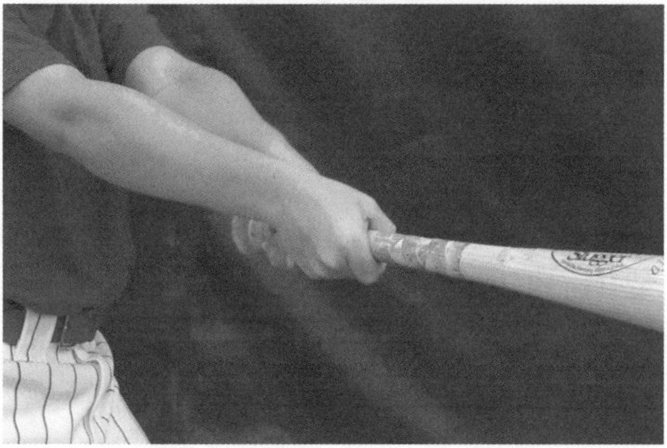

Point of maximum bat speed.
fig. 27

The action of rolling the wrists over is also referred to as "snapping." The harder you snap your wrists, the more bat speed you get.

Quite often your timing is not precise. However, it can still be very good. Within your total swing, the area from where you begin your wrist snap to where you end your wrist snap is the *area* of greatest bat speed (fig. 28). When you hit the ball anywhere in this area, you still get good results.

You cannot always be perfect, but your goal is to *strive* for perfect timing on every swing.

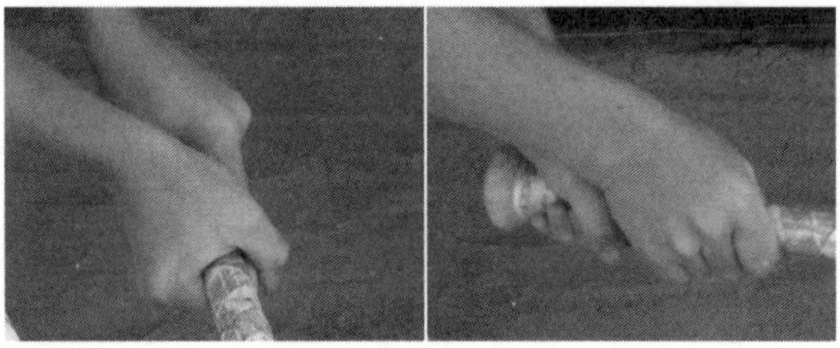

Start of snap. End of snap.
Area of great bat speed.
fig. 28

- **Body Weight.** In your stance, you place 60% of your weight on your back foot and 40% on the front. As you swing, shift some of your weight onto your front foot. Make contact with the same amount of weight on each foot, 50%-50%. This allows you to maintain great balance and throws a little more power into your swing.

  Some coaches make the mistake of teaching young kids to move the body forward *too much* as they step and swing. This just does not work. When all of your body weight ends up directly over the front foot, your swing is locked up. You must keep enough weight back, in order to turn your hips and body properly. When you step and swing, concentrate on turning and not lunging forward.

  Now there have been some great "front-foot hitters" in baseball. Two of my childhood heroes, Hank Aaron and Ernie Banks, come to mind. When hitting the ball, they placed a lot of weight on the front foot, while sliding the back foot away from the plate. However, they stayed behind the ball and did not lunge forward. *Most hitters are better able to maintain good fundamentals and take a complete swing by distributing their weight evenly.*

- **Hitting the Ball Out in Front.** Now let's talk about the importance of "hitting the ball out in front," *before it gets to you.* If you focus on doing this, it will be much easier to apply many of the fundamentals you are learning.

When you *hit the ball out in front*, all of your weight is behind the ball and driving into it. You have turned the foot, knee, and hips, and your arms are extended. In short, you are in your most powerful position.

Be aware, however, that not every ball is meant to be hit out in front of you. The location of the pitch determines where the ball should be hit.

There is a 2-part formula for knowing where to make contact with the ball. *The more inside the pitch, the more out in front you should hit it. The more outside the pitch, the closer you should let it get to you (figs. 29a, b, & c).* Following this formula allows you to contact the ball with the most solid part of your bat.

The exception to the formula is called **"inside-outing."** Instead of hitting an inside pitch out in front, you wait until the ball reaches you and hit it to the opposite field. You may wait intentionally, or you may be late on the pitch. When you swing, keep your hands in close to your body and make contact with your bat *behind* your hands (fig. 30). This keeps you from hitting the ball on or near the handle and getting "jammed."

Sometimes inside-outing just happens, but it can also be learned and used as a strategy. Inside-outing is a valuable tool for right-handed batters on the "hit and run" play—a runner is moved from first to third with just a single.

Inside pitch.
fig. 29a
Where to make contact, figs. 29a, b, & c.

Middle of the plate pitch.
fig. 29b

Outside pitch.
fig. 29c

Inside-out swing.
fig. 30

It is harder to hit with as much power to the opposite field. If you are inside-outing, you get little wrist action. If you are hitting a pitch on the outside corner, you must let the pitch get closer to you in order to reach it. As a result, you get less body and turn behind your swing. You cannot hit that pitch out in front, unless you "get right on top of the plate"—and that can be dangerous.

If you are hitting a pitch *on the inside corner*, hit the ball out in front but do not straighten your arms all the way out. Keep them bent somewhat and in close to your body. This advanced technique allows you to hit many balls fair that you would have otherwise pulled foul.

- **The Sweet Spot.** Another *major* goal is hitting the ball on the "sweet spot" of the bat. The *sweet spot* is the most solid part of the bat. It is the area of the bat where making contact results in the hardest hit baseballs—and the harder you hit the ball, the better your chance of getting on base.

  The sweet spot is usually located within an area of 5 to 7 inches from the end of the bat and in the middle of the wood grain (fig. 31). When the ball hits the sweet spot, there is very little vibration—it almost feels like you did not hit the ball at all.

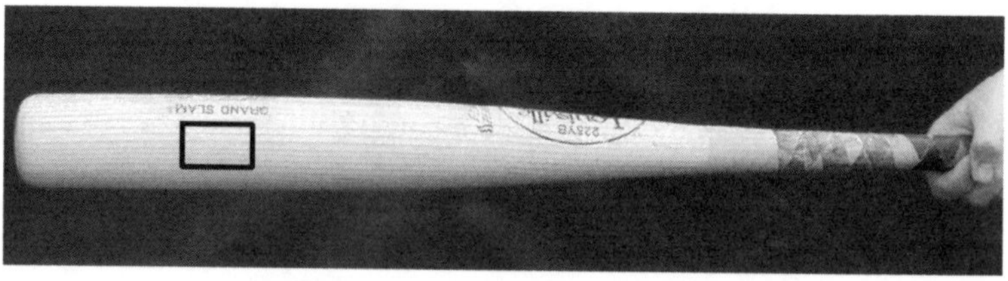

The "sweet spot" of the bat.
fig. 31

- **Head vs. Body.** In hitting, the relationship of your head to the rest of your body is *extremely* important. There is an old saying in baseball, "You can't hit what you can't see." This saying is commonly used to describe how fast a pitcher is throwing, but it also applies here.

  In your stance, you are facing the plate. As you swing, it is natural for your head to turn with the rest of your body. However, when it does, you look away from the plate. You do not see the ball *all the way in.*

  Think of your body as having 2 important parts—your head is one, and the rest of your body is the other. As you swing, you must bring your head in towards the plate while you are turning your body out and away from it.

  If you will master this fundamental and bring your head in with every pitch, you will add many points to your batting average. Meanwhile, as you turn your body, throw everything into your swing—hands, arms, shoulders, hips, knees—everything.

- **Follow-through.** The best and most logical place to finish your swing is up by your shoulder. If you have followed all the fundamentals of the swing, this is where it will end up naturally. You should think in terms of the back shoulder finishing where the front shoulder began.

  Some hitters have a one-handed twist high above the head at the end of the swing, but most hitters do better finishing at the shoulder.

  If you like to let go of the bat with your top hand, make sure you do so *after* snapping your wrists.

The value of thinking about follow-through is that by focusing on where you want to end up, you help ensure your entire swing will be performed correctly.

Wrapping and Hitching

Before closing out this chapter, we must discuss 2 intricate hitting techniques, wrapping and hitching. These techniques or actions can be both good and bad and can affect your hitting in a big way.

Wrapping and hitching are used to create bigger swings and generate more power.

Wrapping. Angling or tilting the top of the bat towards the pitcher is called "wrapping" the bat. *A wrap can be placed in the stance, or it can be used at the start of the swing.* Placing it in the stance usually consumes less time. Most hitters wrap to some degree, either in the stance or during the swing. The drawback is that it takes longer to get the bat around and complete the swing. The bat has to travel a greater distance (figs. 32a & b).

Hitching. A smaller movement made just before a primary movement is called a "hitch." In hitting, the most popular means of hitching is a down-and-up motion of the hands. The hands drop from their starting position—and then come back up (fig. 33). Just as wrapping makes the swing bigger and uses up more time, so does hitching.

Wrapping and Hitching. Some hitters wrap and hitch together. The hands drop from their starting position as the bat wraps—then they come back up (fig. 34). This combination also uses up a lot of time. How much time it uses depends on how big the wrap and hitch are.

Not wrapping.
fig. 32a

Wrapping.
fig. 32b

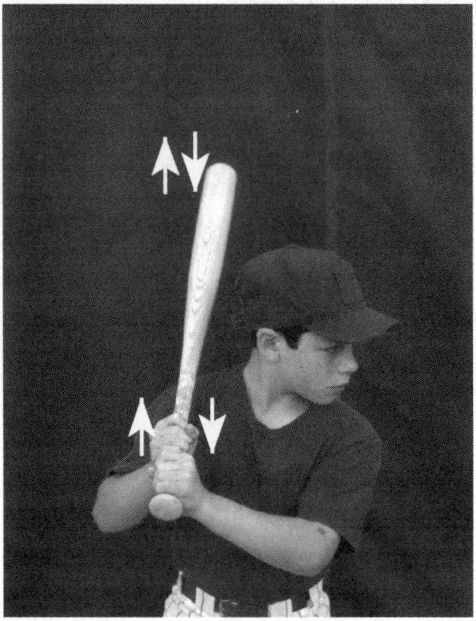

Hitching.
fig. 33

Wrapping
and hitching.
fig. 34

Kansas City Royals third baseman George Brett was one of the greatest hitters ever. He placed a huge wrap in his stance, but did not hitch. Other star hitters like Mike Piazza wrap *during the swing* and do not hitch. Then there are great hitters like Barry Bonds and Jeff Bagwell who use big hitches. Like most players who hitch, they also wrap.

How are hitters able to wrap and hitch? *Since wrapping and hitching make the swing bigger and use up more time, how can players wrap and hitch without being late on the pitch?* They do so by putting the wrap and hitch in motion early. San Francisco Giants left fielder Barry Bonds is in his *wrap and hitch* before the pitcher even releases the ball—his hands have dropped down almost to his waist. As the ball comes in, he brings them back up to the hitting position. By starting early, Bonds is able to wrap and hitch without losing any "bat time."

Hitters with big wraps and hitches are timing not only the ball, but also the pitcher's motion and release point. This is made easier by "knowing" the pitchers and by sometimes "looking for a pitch." Looking for a pitch is guessing what the pitcher will throw. (This will be discussed in chapters 7 and 9.)

The trouble is, not everyone who tries to wrap and hitch big can do it. When starting the swing before seeing the ball, it can be more difficult to start at the right time. Starting too soon can make it difficult or impossible to hold up on a bad pitch, or on a pitch that fools you. Waiting too long to start the swing can result in being "jammed" by an inside fastball, losing power, or hitting the ball foul.

The ability to wrap and hitch depends on a player's timing and strength, along with the things we just mentioned that help make it easier (knowing the pitchers, looking for a pitch).

I do not recommend hitching. However, if you can hitch *and still hit well*, go ahead and hitch.

If you can wrap and still hit well, wrap to the extent you are able. Remember that we placed a small wrap of a few inches in your *best hitting stance* (fig. 15).

The Quick Swing. When you use your *best hitting stance* and swing without wrapping or hitching, you are taking your "quickest swing" possible. You are able to wait and get a great look at the pitch.

Whenever you add something to your *quickest swing*, the swing gets bigger and takes longer to complete. You are forced to start sooner, and you must time the pitcher's motion and release point more precisely. Unless you are extremely talented, you will be fooled more often by the speed and location of the pitch.

Moreover, hitters like Mark McGwire and Moises Alou prove that you can get a good look, take a quick swing, and still generate plenty of speed and power. ***The quickest swing is the best approach for most young hitters.***

Bat Weight. What if you are in your *best hitting stance*, using your *quickest swing*, and you still cannot get around on the fastball? Many young players today face this problem when entering high school and are required by rule to swing a heavier bat.

You can use a technique I learned from my San Francisco Giants hitting instructor, Hank Sauer. Change your *best hitting stance* slightly. Tilt your bat so that it is angled back towards the backstop, in the opposite direction of a wrapped bat (fig. 35).

This technique saves even more time than simply not wrapping. You may sacrifice a little power, but you must be able to get around on the ball. As you develop more strength, you can work your way back.

Using bat angle to create a quicker swing.
fig. 35

Now that the entire swing has been explained, lock this picture in your mind—you are driving quickly from your stance to the point of contact in a continuous and powerful motion. You snap your wrists hard and follow all the way through (fig. 36).

You now have all the knowledge necessary for developing a great swing—you know what makes up the *Major League Swing*. Yet, knowing how to develop a great swing is only the beginning.

The swing.
fig. 36

7

GAME SITUATION HITTING

It has long been said that baseball is a game of inches. Is this ever true! Just 1/4 of an inch is often the difference between a double and a home run, between a foul ball and a strikeout. A little slip-up in any of your hitting skills can result in that 1/4 of an inch difference. Therefore, you must always concentrate on your hitting skills.

However, *physical* skills alone are not enough. There are also skills of the mind. Baseball is a thinking person's game, and your success also depends on your *mental* approach to the game. When you reach a level in baseball where the players all have good *physical* skills, knowing *how* to play the game will help you prevail.

When hitting in a game situation, you must ask the following:

1) What does the pitcher throw?
2) What are the pitcher's tendencies?
3) What are the game circumstances?
4) What are the playing conditions?

What Does the Pitcher Throw?

For Little Leaguers, this is usually not a problem. Most pitchers at this age throw 1 pitch—whatever fastball they have. However, as you get older and play in higher levels of baseball, almost every pitcher has 2, 3, or even 4 different pitches. The most common pitches are the fastball, curveball, slider, sinker, and change-up. There are also specialty pitches like the screwball, knuckleball, forkball (split-finger), knuckle-curve, and even the illegal spitball.

Defining the more common pitches

The following definitions describe a right-handed batter facing a right-handed pitcher (and a left-handed batter facing a left-handed pitcher).

A pitch thrown "straight and hard" is a **fastball**. The speed of a fastball gives you little time to react. Fastballs can be thrown with different grips and release points.

A slow speed, tight-spinning pitch that breaks down and away is a **curveball**. Its slow speed and big break fool you.

A fast speed, corkscrew-spinning pitch that breaks down and away just enough to make you miss it is a **slider**. It is thrown hard and fools you by appearing to be a fastball.

A fairly fast, side-spinning pitch that moves down and in a little is a **sinker**. Its downward movement produces a lot of ground balls.

A slow moving pitch, thrown with the motion of a fastball, is a **change-up**. The change in speed fools you. Change-ups can be thrown with several different grips. A change-up thrown with the motion and spin of an overhand fastball is extremely effective, because it looks so much like a fastball.

In order to be a successful hitter, you must "learn" the pitchers. Believe me, they make mental notes and study all of your at-bats. Their goal is to throw pitches that you do not hit well. In turn, you must prepare for them. When you go to the plate, you must know what pitches a pitcher has in order to know what you are up against.

For example, what happens if there are 2 strikes on you and the pitcher snaps off a curveball that you did not know he had? You will probably be so fooled that you will watch it cut down and into the plate for strike 3. If you know he has this pitch, you will be more prepared to get at least some type of cut at it.

You must also pay attention to what the pitches do. Does the pitcher's fastball rise, sink, or come in straight? How much does his curve break? Once you know what the pitcher throws, you should concentrate on learning his tendencies.

What are the Pitcher's Tendencies?

If a pitcher has a variety of pitches and mixes them up well, he is going to be tough to hit. However, many pitchers like to throw a specific pitch in a specific situation. We say that the pitcher has a *tendency* to throw a given pitch in that situation. A pitcher can also have a tendency to throw a particular pitch almost exclusively, regardless of the situation. That pitch could be a fastball, a curve, or any other pitch that gets hitters out.

Before you go up to bat, study the pitcher's tendencies. If the 2 hitters before you got fastballs on their first 2 strikes and were struck out with curves, you have a pretty good indication of what you can expect. You will probably get some fastballs early in the count and that same curve with 2 strikes on you. The pitcher has shown a tendency to "get ahead" with the fastball and use the curve as his "out pitch."

If you see that a pitcher shows a tendency to throw mostly curves to everyone, look for that curve on your first 2 strikes. When you get it in a good enough location, crush it. Likewise, if a pitcher is throwing all fastballs, *or if the fastball is the only pitch he can throw for a strike,* why look for anything else?

Be aware that game circumstances can also affect a pitcher's tendencies.

Game Circumstances

Game circumstances include things like the count, the score, the inning, where the runners are, and other related factors. Game circumstances help determine how you should play the game.

For example: It is late in a close game—a man is on second—and there are no outs. In this situation, you are expected to "move the runner over." If you can get the runner to third base with 1 out, he will have several ways of scoring when the next batter comes up. Your goal is to hit the ball to the right side. This enables the runner to advance on a ground ball, a hit, or a deep fly ball. You can even bunt him over. You "sacrifice" your at-bat to help the team win.

Another example: With the first baseman holding a runner on, there is a much wider area on the right side for a ground ball to go through for a hit. If you can hit the ball well to right field, you may want to aim for it.

A further example: Runners are on second and third—no one is on first—and you are the batter. You must be aware that a good pitcher will try to make you "fish" for a bad pitch. Walking you does not hurt him because it sets up a force-out at any base. On the other hand, if you are not hitting well, you may expect to get some *better* pitches to hit—especially if the next batter *is* hitting well. With less than 2 outs, the pitcher would try to get you out and walk the "hot" hitter to set up the force.

These are just a few examples of situations and strategies you learn through experience.

The On-Deck Circle. Many players just swing without purpose in the on-deck circle—they turn their heads out with their practice swings. *Why* is this bad? It is said that **baseball is a game of repetition**. This means that when you practice something over and over, it becomes automatic—you do it that way every time without even having to think about it.

Use your warm-up swings to reinforce good technique, not poor technique. Bring your head in to the plate, even when you are just taking practice swings.

Hitting with the Count. Your mental approach to hitting is greatly affected by the count. Being ahead in the count (more balls than strikes) usually gives you the advantage. You are not in danger of striking out, so you can pick the pitch you want to hit. Being behind in the count (more strikes than balls) usually gives the pitcher the advantage. He is not in danger of walking you, so he does not have to give you a good pitch to hit. A full count of 3-2 is not considered being ahead in the count, because you are down to your last strike.

Let's look at how **you can mentally frame your strike zone**, according to how many strikes there are on you.

With no strikes, you should be looking to hit a ball that is within a very select area (fig. 37).

Your strike zone with no strikes on you.
fig. 37

With 1 strike on you, the area gets larger (fig. 38).

Your strike zone with 1 strike on you.
fig. 38

With 2 strikes on you, you must protect the plate (fig. 39).

Your strike zone with 2 strikes on you.
fig. 39

These strike zones that *you* establish help keep you from swinging at bad pitches "early" in the count and help remind you to protect the plate "late" in the count. They may be affected by the umpiring. If an umpire is calling "everything" a strike, your strike zones must get bigger. If he is not calling "anything," you can make them smaller.

You can also use the count to **"look for a pitch."** When you do so, you *assume* the pitcher will throw a specific pitch. For example, you could *look* for a fastball, or a curve, and so on. *It is easier to time a pitch that you are looking for*—make your strike zones a little bigger and attack the ball.

You can change the pitch you look for as the count changes. For example, you may look for a fastball with a 1-0 count—then, with the count 1-1, you may decide to look for a breaking pitch. You can change with every pitch, but you do not have to.

Another strategy is to look for a pitch for a given number of strikes. Sometimes it is worth the gamble to look for the pitch you want on your first 2 strikes. Of course, if you do not get it, you could end up behind in the count. Looking for your pitch on the third strike is very risky.

When you are ahead in the count, many pitchers will throw their fastball. They have more control with it, and they do not want to walk you. Look for a fastball and rip it. You are also more likely to get a *good* fastball to hit—the pitcher knows that if he aims for the corner, he could miss and fall even further behind in the count.

Although many pitchers throw fastballs when they are behind in the count, you cannot *always* depend on it. A pitcher's success lies in keeping you off balance. If you are facing a pitcher with command (control) of all his pitches, or if you are a hot hitter, you may not get that 2-0 fastball. A pitcher with great control can throw you any pitch at any time. Therefore, use the count to "look fastball," but also consider the pitcher and his abilities.

When you look for a specific pitch or pitch location, and you get either one, it is called **"getting your pitch."** When you *get your pitch,* you must make good on it. You must hit it hard. The more you advance in baseball, the more this applies. In the Big Leagues, you may only get 1 good pitch to hit per at-bat. The players who always hit that one pitch hard are your .300 hitters.

With 2 strikes on you, be prepared to hit the pitcher's best pitch. If his best pitch is a fastball, make sure you are ready to take a quick swing. If his best pitch is a slow curve, think "wait, but be quick if it is a fastball."

Playing Conditions

Playing conditions can also affect your approach to hitting. From a hitter's standpoint, you are mostly concerned with wind, light, and moisture.

Check out the wind. The ball will carry or "hang up" and fade depending on which direction the wind is blowing. If there is a strong wind blowing in, you should use a more level swing and go for line drives. Also, be more selective at the plate. Settle for the walk.

If the wind is blowing out, use your regular swing. However, be aware that the pitcher's ball will move more with the wind against him. Curves and sliders will break bigger, sinkers will sink more, and so on.

Sometimes you have to bat in a sunlight-to-shadow situation. The pitcher throws the ball—you see it part of the way—then it enters a shadowed area where it is more difficult to see. Breaking balls like curves and sliders are particularly tough to hit, because it is hard to "pick up" the change in direction of the ball. Still, your best course of action in this situation is also the safest—look to hit the fastball, and adjust to all other pitches.

If you are batting in a wet, sloppy batter's box, you must adjust accordingly. Widen your stance a little. When you swing, concentrate on turning and not striding. If you are in loose, soft sand, do the same—widen your stance and shorten your stride.

8

HITTING THE FASTBALL

There are several different kinds of fastballs. **When hitting most fastballs, your focus is on timing, being quick, and taking a good swing.** *A smart hitter also learns to recognize the different fastballs by appearance, movement, and the pitcher's delivery.* If you know how a pitcher's fastball moves, you have a better chance of being successful at the plate.

Fastballs can move up, down, in, or out, depending on how the ball is gripped and thrown. There are 2 basic ways to grip a fastball—with fingers across the seams (*cross-seam fastball*), and with fingers in line with the seams (*with-the-seams fastball*).

Cross-seam Fastball. Most pitchers throw a *cross-seam fastball*—especially in higher levels of baseball. Because of the way it spins, the cross-seam fastball has a very solid appearance. Cross-seam fastballs are thrown mostly overhand, but they can also be thrown sidearm or "submarine." They come in straight and hard. Concentrate on seeing the ball and being quick.

When a cross-seam fastball is thrown overhand with superior speed, it has a rising effect and is called a *rising fastball*. It is also called a **power fastball**, because it overpowers most hitters.

Although you know which way this power fastball moves, the rising fastball is still a big problem—it crosses the plate a few inches higher than the fastballs you are used to seeing. It can seem like you are "right on the pitch," when you are not. You find yourself swinging below the ball and missing, or you just get a piece of it and pop up. When this happens, you must adjust.

The adjustment you must make to the rising fastball is more mental than physical. Since you are swinging lower than where the ball is, you must change the location of your swing. ***Start by swinging a little higher than where you see the ball. If you need to, increase the distance between where you swing and where you see the ball, until you are making good contact again.*** This will require concentration and discipline, but it is what you must do to hit this power fastball. Keep in mind that you are raising your swing, not changing it. Concentrate also on being extra quick.

With-the-seams Fastball. Some pitchers throw a *with-the-seams fastball*. Because of the way it spins, this pitch does not have the solid appearance of a cross-seam fastball. A with-the-seams fastball can be thrown overhand, sidearm, or submarine and can move in, out, or down. When thrown overhand, this fastball is more likely to move in or out. When thrown sidearm or submarine, it is more likely to move down. It does not usually move a lot, but even a little ball movement makes hitting tougher. Quite often a with-the-seams fastball just comes in straight and hard. Concentrate on seeing the ball and being quick.

When pitchers throw a with-the-seams fastball with more sidespin, it usually moves down and is called a **sinker**. *Sinkers* can be thrown fairly hard, or they can be thrown at slower speeds. Because they are usually thrown slower than regular fastballs and move down, we will discuss hitting them in the next chapter.

9

OFF-SPEED PITCHES AND WAYS TO MENTALLY APPROACH HITTING

Off-speed pitches are pitches thrown at slower speeds. Their purpose is to disrupt the timing of the hitter. Off-speed pitches often frustrate even the best hitters in baseball. The most common off-speed pitches are change-ups and slow curves. However, any pitch thrown slower than a pitcher's best fastball can be considered an off-speed pitch.

When comparing pitches by speed, the fastest pitch is the fastball. The slider, sinker, and hard knuckle-curve come next, followed by the forkball (split-finger). Change-ups, curveballs, and screwballs are slow pitches, and the forkball can also be thrown at a slower speed. The knuckleball is the slowest pitch of all.

Whether hitting off-speed pitches or fastballs, your success depends on your ability to:

1) Recognize the pitch.
2) Adjust to the pitch.

How you go about recognizing and adjusting depends on how you are mentally approaching the pitch.

There are 2 basic ways to mentally approach hitting any pitch. One way is to **"see the ball and hit it."** The other way is to **"look for a pitch."** When you *see the ball and hit it*, you look for the ball and react to what it does. When you *look for a pitch*, you assume what the pitch will be and plan your swing accordingly (chap. 7).

See the Ball and Hit it

Recognizing the Pitch. When you *see the ball and hit it,* recognize the pitch by picking up the ball as soon as possible—try to determine how fast the ball is traveling, the type of spin it has, and the direction it is moving in.

Adjusting to the Pitch. When using the *see the ball and hit it* approach, you must think of being quick enough to hit a fastball and composed enough to wait on an off-speed pitch.

Start by being ready for anything. When you recognize a fastball, be quick and use what you learned in the previous chapter.

When you recognize an off-speed pitch, do not change your swing. Keep your same great swing, only change when and where you use it. You know that these pitches are slower and move down, so do not swing where you see the ball 15 feet out in front of you. ***Wait longer and swing where the ball will be when it gets to you.*** *Lower your swing as a whole—do not change your swing fundamentals.* This is the same mental technique used to hit the rising fastball, only now you are adjusting to downward movement of the ball.

Sometimes you get fooled at the plate. When *seeing the ball and hitting it,* you get fooled when you believe the pitch is a fastball and it is really something else. It is hard to adjust once you have been fooled, especially to change-ups, sliders, and splitters. However, you can sometimes adjust to slow curves.

Practice being fooled by the curve by *imagining* you are up to bat. You see a fastball—you step forward and start your swing—then you realize the pitch is a curve. Stop your swing and bring it back just a little. Take a quick, up-and-down step with your front foot and *restart* the swing. Do not take a second step forward or you will be overstriding. Concentrate on snapping your wrists with power. You should also practice flinching away from the plate and moving back quickly to swing.

Look for a Pitch

Recognizing the Pitch. When you *look for a pitch,* recognize the pitch just as you did when seeing the ball and hitting it. Only now, you are already assuming what the pitch will be.

Adjusting to the Pitch. When using the *look for a pitch* approach, you *plan* your timing and swing. Rather than *waiting* to adjust, you anticipate the speed and movement of the ball. Now you have a great chance of hitting the ball hard if you get what you want.

When you *look for* a fastball and *recognize late* that the pitch is off-speed, do not try to "hold up" your swing—you are too far *ahead* of the pitch. A swing and a miss is better than slowing down your swing and hitting the ball softly for an out.

When you *look for* an off-speed pitch and *recognize late* that the pitch is a fastball, do not swing—you are too far *behind* in timing the pitch.

With 2 strikes on you, just see the ball and hit it. Protect the plate by using your wide strike zone.

Suspect a Pitch

There is a third way to mentally approach hitting a pitch, called **"suspecting a pitch."** *Suspecting a pitch* is a combination of the first 2 basic ways. You are 50% *looking for a pitch*, and 50% *seeing the ball and hitting it.* Suspect that you will get one pitch, over the other pitches the pitcher has, but do not commit totally to it. Leave yourself enough time to adjust at the last split second in case you do not get the pitch you are suspecting.

A very talented hitter can suspect a fastball and still wait long enough to hit an off-speed pitch well. An extremely talented hitter can suspect an off-speed pitch and still be quick enough to get around on the fastball.

Now that you know how to hit a variety of pitches, you must be able to apply your knowledge. Whether you can will depend on several factors.

10

NATURAL ABILITY

Natural ability is *the ability one is born with.* It can vary greatly from person to person. People with a lot of natural ability are able to excel (as in baseball) with very little difficulty. They just seem to "have it," while others do not. Again, few players have the natural ability necessary for reaching the Major Leagues. *However*, you should consider the following before you drop out, especially if you are a young or beginning player having a little trouble.

It is known that *people often develop at different rates*, both physically and mentally. At the age of 9, Johnny may be a better ballplayer than Jimmy. At the age of 13, Jimmy overtakes Johnny. Jimmy just took a little longer to grow and learn.

Some people also continue to learn and improve their skills after others have reached their limits. Many young players barely make a high school or college team, but continue to get much better each year. Others who were rated higher may improve very little during the same period of time. It is hard to predict who will be the best graduating player.

The same can even happen in the Major Leagues. By the age of 37, most players have retired. Yet, Cardinals center fielder Lou Brock set a new Major League stolen base record at the age of 37. Edgar Martinez, slugger for the 2000 Seattle Mariners, also had his best season ever at the age of 37 when he batted .324, with 37 home runs and 145 RBI.

Of course, *quality of instruction* can make all the difference in the world. Learning the wrong fundamentals and techniques can make a player *appear* to have poor ability. *So, if you have not been using the fundamentals and techniques in this book,* ***start now!***

When hitting a baseball, hand-eye coordination is a big factor. There are players with great form and great swings who are unable to make good contact with the ball. (Form simply means the motions of the body.) These players have trouble with their hand-eye coordination. Hand-eye coordination can be improved with practice, but how much it can improve depends on each person's natural ability.

Natural ability is surely necessary, but it is not everything. Although it takes natural ability to be a great player, there are other individual qualities that can make up for some lack of natural ability.

In the upcoming chapters, we look at some of these qualities.

11

DESIRE AND LOVE OF THE GAME

When striving to reach any goal, desire is the most important factor of all. Without it, you can never be the best you can be. **In order to achieve success, a burning desire *to* succeed is usually necessary.**

In baseball, we say: "You've got to love this game!" What good is being the best hitter in the world if you do not want to play? There are many athletes who had the ability to play on a college or professional baseball team but never did.

When my professional career was over, I played a little softball around town and was amazed at some of the great swings, gloves, and arms that I saw. I often found myself saying, "This guy should have played professionally."

I am sure that some of these athletes were forced into the situation of having to work at a young age to support a family. Others faced different circumstances beyond their control that kept them from playing baseball. However, most of them lacked at least one of the ingredients that makes up **the formula for success**. I have found that formula to be: **Love + Desire = Success.** Of course there are other *keys* to success, but let's look at this simple formula.

First, find something that you love to do. Add a great desire to succeed, and you end up with your best chance of being successful. If you *love* what you are doing but do not have that burning desire to succeed, you will come up short. You will not put enough effort into it. If you have the *desire* to succeed but you are doing something that you do not like—or that you do not believe in—you are also bound to fail. It takes love *and* desire to rise to the top.

Success rarely comes before failure. In fact, we often define success as the end result of overcoming our failures, as well as the obstacles blocking our road to success.

This is especially true in baseball. You must survive hitting slumps, injuries, and other discouraging situations. One day you are a hero—the next day you are a goat. You may even have great seasons, but receive little or no reward. At the professional level, they tell you there is no room at the top—the players above you are also doing well. You have to be mentally tough enough to hang in there until something opens up. You must be able to put disappointment behind you and play with confidence every day.

12

MOTIVATION AND DETERMINATION

No matter what your goal, motivation and determination are among the keys necessary to achieve success.

Motivation is anything that inspires you to take action. You never know what might motivate you in a positive way. It could be the desire to succeed or impress people. Perhaps you seek to gain the respect of others. You can be motivated by love. If you fail at something, you may just want to prove you can do it. How about wanting to be the best in the world at what you do—or simply wanting to better yourself? You can even turn anger into motivation that helps you to achieve something positive.

What about in baseball when a pitcher strikes you out? If striking out makes you feel bad and motivates you, you will not give up—you will continue to try hard.

With this approach, you should do well in youth baseball. However, if your goal is to play on a college or professional team, you will probably need to do more.

There are different *degrees* of motivation. Motivation helps give you the desire to succeed, but being able to compete at a very high level requires more than just *some* motivation. If you are truly motivated, you will do whatever it takes. **Your motivation and desire will give you determination.** When you are *determined* to be successful, you will practice and practice until you *can* be.

When you think about the pitcher who struck you out, you will say to yourself, "Yeah, you got me this time, but I'll be seeing you again."

How well you do and how far you go depend greatly on the degree of motivation and determination you have. You will never know how good you can be, unless you give it a good enough try. Sometimes the pitcher who gets you out is just one step ahead of you at the time.

I remember facing a lefty in Pony League All-Star play who threw harder than anything I had ever seen. I was overmatched, but I found out the following year that I could rise to that level of competition.

13

HOW TO PRACTICE HITTING

"What you do in practice is what you do in the game." This is what one of my coaches told me years ago, and I have found these words to be true.

Your success as a hitter depends on what you practice—you must practice good fundamentals to become a skilled player. However, ***how* you practice is also very important**.

Let's break away from hitting for a moment for a good illustration of this point.

It is infield practice, and you are taking ground balls. If you are fooling around and lobbing your throws softly to first base, what do you think will happen in the game when you are suddenly caught in the position of having to throw out a speedy runner? You will probably throw the ball away. You may even hurt your arm if you did not warm up properly.

The lesson here is to throw the ball hard—even in practice. What you do in practice *is* what you do in the game.

The same applies to hitting. If you take giant strides and pull your head out while overswinging in practice, what will you likely do in the game?

How about your timing? If you will be batting against a pitcher who throws 70 mph, how much good will it do to take batting practice at 40 mph? *Again*, base your practice on what you will need to do in the game.

Any time you practice, it is vitally important that you first warm up properly. (This is discussed in the next chapter.)

Ways to Practice Hitting

There are 4 basic ways to practice hitting.

1) Off the tee
2) Soft toss
3) Pitching machine
4) Live pitching

Off the Tee. Hitting *off the tee* is a method of practice used by many people, including some Major Leaguers. It can be very helpful in working on hand-eye coordination. Sometimes a player's technique is good, but he keeps missing the ball. Hitting off the tee may help place his swing in the right location.

I did not use the tee for several reasons. First, I never had a serious problem of swinging and missing. Secondly, I found that I could not *prepare for the pitch* as I did in a game—the tee and ball were in the way of my practice swings.

However, my biggest complaint against the tee is that you cannot put the ball on one in a game—you have to hit a moving object.

The tee is okay for "lining up" your swing, but it does little for your timing.

Soft Toss. Another method of practice used for hitting is *soft toss*. Someone kneels or stands on your oped side about 6 feet away and softly tosses the baseballs out in front of you. You hit them "straight away" and not in the direction of the tosser (fig. 40). You can get in a lot of swings in a batting cage, because you do not have to spend your time rounding up baseballs.

Soft toss.
fig. 40

I like this method because you can set up just like you prepare for the pitch in a game. The ball is at least moving, so you are getting the visual practice of hitting a moving object. You are also working on adjusting your swing to a degree, as the ball can be tossed with different arcs and in different locations. If you do not have a person to toss, hold the bat with one hand and toss the ball up with your other.

Pitching Machines. Pitching machines are good because you can fix the distance, speed, and location of the ball to closely simulate a game situation. They also throw pretty good curveballs. However, pitching machines do not throw all pitches exactly the way humans do.

One machine that threw great fastballs was the old "Iron Mike." We had an *Iron Mike* at Brevard Junior College in 1969, and it was used almost every day. *Iron Mike* threw with a mechanical arm that came up and over the top. A fastball from *Iron Mike* had the spin and movement of a real overhand fastball. It was almost as good as hitting off a real pitcher.

The advantage of the pitching machine is that it does not get a sore arm, and it does not get tired. However, to practice hitting off a pitching machine, you need the machine—and they can be expensive.

Live Pitching. *There is nothing better than "live" pitching.* Only a real person can throw exactly like a real person. But let the coaches do the *live* pitching—not everyday players. The risk of hurting an arm is too great, especially when throwing a lot of hard pitches or breaking balls.

Additional Ways to Practice Hitting

There are 2 additional ways to practice hitting. Hitting in a real game is one way—*shadow hitting* is another.

Real Game Hitting. We usually think of playing games and practicing as two different things. Yet, when you bat in a game, you are certainly practicing your hitting. This kind of practice becomes known as experience and is perhaps the most important kind of practice. (Experience is discussed in chapter 14.)

Shadow Hitting. What if there is only you and your bat? Be a shadow hitter. Just as a boxer shadow boxes, so can you *shadow hit*.

When shadow boxing, a fighter throws sequences of organized, coordinated punches at an imaginary foe. He does not just throw punches aimlessly and without purpose.

When I was 13 years old, I created *shadow hitting* (at least for myself) as a means of practicing when I had no team or friend to play ball with. I would work on my swing in the front or back yard by looking at my reflection in a low window or inexpensive stand-up mirror. (If you are not an adult, get permission to do this—and do not let go of the bat!)

Take a stance so that you see yourself as the pitcher does. Check out your stance. Look for hands in the hitting position and correct bat angle. Bend the knees and lean over at the waist, just as you do when batting. View your swing as you hit imaginary pitches in every location—low, in, high, and away. Snap your wrists according to where the pitch is—inside, middle of the plate, or outside. Make sure your swing angle is a slight uppercut where you would meet the ball. Take some swings in slow motion, so you can really study everything. Practice being fooled and adjusting to off-speed pitches.

Now turn 90 degrees and view yourself from your open side (like in soft toss). Check your stance again. Look for correct weight distribution and bat angle. Make sure the front shoulder and elbow are lower than the back ones and that the back elbow is pointing at the catcher's head. Watch yourself as you swing at all types of pitches. Make sure your swing angle is a slight uppercut where you would meet the ball. Do the same things you did from out of the front stance.

Stop a swing at the point of contact, freezing in your mind that you want to hit that inside or middle-of-the-plate pitch out in front of you. Look to see that the back foot and knee are turned in.

All serious hitters should use shadow hitting as a method of practice. It is a great way to reinforce good form and technique.

Practice—The More the Better

The best advice on practice is *the more the better*!

Consider 2 individuals with the same amount of ability. One practices for 2 hours, 1 day a week. The other practices for 2 hours, 4 days a week. Who will more likely fulfill his potential?

Now I do not say practice 8 hours a day and never take time off during the year. I have a friend who practices his 14-year-old son almost every day of the year. He tells me "Hey, if you're not practicing, someone else is." Hopefully, his son will not sustain an injury. The key is to practice as much as you can, but give yourself a little time off once in a while.

At the end of Chapter 10, I said that other qualities could make up for some lack of natural ability. We have discussed some of these qualities—like desire, love, motivation, and determination. Now we can add **practice and hard work** to the list.

14

PHYSICAL CONDITIONING

Physical conditioning plays an important role in the performance of a baseball player. Always make sure that your level and means of physical conditioning are approved by your doctor. This rule applies to fitness programs, as well as sports and regular exercise. A program or routine that is good for one person may not be good for another.

Size and strength are very important. It is a big advantage to be strong and powerful if you can hit. However, power is also the product of great coordination and timing. There are guys bigger and stronger than Luis Gonzalez who have not hit 57 home runs in a Major League season!

Getting in Shape

After resting between seasons, you should take special care in how you get back into "playing shape."

A Little Leaguer who plays sports at school is probably always in good running shape, while a professional player may not be as active year-round. No matter what your age, remember this: The longer the period of inactivity, the more care you must take in getting back into playing shape.

When getting back in shape, first work on your legs and wind. We always started off the college or professional season by jogging for distance to regain leg strength and breathing endurance. Do this for at least a few days, or for as long as a week or so. Then it is time to get into sprints.

Just as you jog before you sprint, you must never start a season by throwing or swinging your hardest on the first day—doing so could result in injury. Throw half speed and swing easy. Practice every day for about a week or so, working just a little harder each day. Then you should be ready to get serious.

I am a firm believer in stretching and warming up before playing. Your doctor and most coaches can show you some good stretching exercises and calisthenics. Stretch and do calisthenics for at least 5 minutes before playing—this will help prevent a needless injury.

I find it particularly important to stretch the hamstrings well. Even if you are running late, always stretch the hamstrings. A pulled hamstring muscle is an injury that can usually be prevented by stretching and warming up properly. It is also one that can take a long time to heal. I pulled a hamstring in college, and it took more than a month to recover from that injury. *Never* neglect stretching your hamstrings before playing.

There are several ways to stretch hamstrings—use the one your doctor recommends. One way is to keep your legs straight and touch your toes. This can be done from the standing or sitting position—you can place your feet together, apart, or one crossed over the other. If you cannot reach your toes, stop your stretch short of the point where you begin to feel too much pain. Most players still use this method.

Another way to stretch your hamstrings is to stand on one leg and place the other on a table or bench (toe up). Bend forward at the waist to increase your stretch, but stop short of the point where you begin to feel too much pain.

You can also stretch hamstrings in a way that is easier on your back—but you will need a partner. Lie on your back, while your partner kneels by your side and places one hand on the front of your nearest thigh, just above the knee. With the other hand, he/she holds the foot or ankle of that leg and raises the leg up straight, but not to the point of too much pain. In this manner, the hamstring is stretched with the back straight and relaxed.

A great variation of this method is to keep the leg moving in a circular motion as you raise it up and bring it back down. Keep the speed easy and do the number of repetitions you need to get loose.

Some players hold their stretches in place for about 6 seconds, while others feel it is okay to "bounce" at the stretch point. Use the method your doctor recommends.

Preparing for Practices and Games

Even when you are in good physical shape, you must continue to take care of yourself.

My 11-year-old son stretches his hamstrings and hangs from a pull-up bar before we go to the park. At the ball field, do the recommended 5 minutes of stretching and calisthenics to loosen up your neck, arms, back, waist, and legs.

Next, jog a lap around the field. Then warm up your arm. *Always* throw easy at first and build up speed. Your arm needs its own warm-up time.

Finally, run about five 30-yard sprints. Use the "build up" system here too. Run your first sprint at 75% and work your way up to 100% on the last one.

For Strength—Exercise the Motion Required

The Batting Ring. I recommend a simple exercise for strengthening your swing. Put a batting ring on your bat and swing it. Concentrate on form, technique, and wrist snap. How often you exercise with the ring depends on your baseball schedule. Every other day is a good routine.

The number of swings you take depends on your size and strength. My son takes 10 medium warm-up swings. Then he takes 10 hard swings, concentrating on wrist snap. You should start out with the number of swings you think you can easily handle. If you feel you can do more, go ahead. If you feel like you are *losing* strength in your arms, or like your arms are too sore, you should cut back a little.

Do not use the ring to exercise on the day before a game. Your muscles need time to rebuild. On game day, take 3 or 4 swings with the ring before each at-bat. This temporarily pumps up your strength and makes your swing quicker.

Exercise the Motions You Use. I like the ring because it is not too heavy and because *it builds up strength specific to the swing.*

Consider a field goal kicker in football. His success at kicking long distance field goals does not come from running or lifting weights. These exercises condition the body, but the kicker's success comes from kicking the football—*it comes from strengthening the muscles and coordination for the motion required.* Many people run and lift weights, but few can kick long field goals. (Weights *can* be of help when used to strengthen the *kicking motion.*)

Many big, muscular people cannot throw a baseball properly. Yet, I remember batting against Ron Guidry of the Yankees. At 165 lbs., his fastball was hardly visible!

Exercise the motions required for the skill—and remember that playing your game strengthens your game!

15

EXPERIENCE

In baseball, the word "experience" has several meanings. It can mean the number of organized *games* a player has played. It can mean the number of *years* a player has played organized baseball. It can also mean the number of games or years played *at a given level* of organized baseball.

Organized baseball is baseball that is structured and played by teams in official leagues.

When you practice, you are also getting experience. Still, you are judged by how well you play in organized games, not practice. If you practice for 5 years, but play no games, people will say you have no experience.

You may hear a television commentator talk about a rookie Major Leaguer needing more experience, even though the player has played baseball for most of his life. The commentator is talking about experience playing at the Major League level.

There is a big difference between practicing and playing in an organized game. In game play, wins and losses are recorded, as are hitting, pitching, and fielding statistics. As a hitter, you are facing the pitcher's "best stuff." The intensity level is high because this is when it counts. Throughout all of this, you must play relaxed in order to do your best. Only through experience will you succeed in doing so.

How Much Experience Do You Need?

There is an old saying: **"There's no substitute for experience."** You need all the experience you can get!

Let's illustrate this with an analogy. Consider speaking before an audience. I will never forget the speech class I took at Brevard Junior College. When the day came for each student to give a two-minute speech before the class, I was a nervous wreck—and I was nervous for a very long time, because I was almost the last speaker.

When I gave my speech, my heart pounded, my knees grew weak, and my hands perspired. I did not deliver a very good speech that day. Since then, the quality of my speeches has improved. I found that the more speeches I gave, the easier it became to relax and do well. I just needed more experience. The same applies to baseball.

Although I experienced a few nervous times in baseball, I never felt as bad going to the plate as I did in speech class. I hope you never do either. If you ever take a speech class, raise your hand, go first and get it over with!

Don't Give Up Too Soon

Do not get discouraged if you do not succeed right away in a higher level of play. Remember what we talked about earlier and give yourself a little time.

I recall that Dodgers first baseman Steve Garvey was not an immediate success when he was first called up to the Major Leagues. He was sent back down to AAA baseball for a while, but did very well after being called up again. He went on to become one of the best Major League hitters ever. In 1974, Steve was named the National League's Most Valuable Player.

You will never know what you can achieve until you have gained a substantial amount of experience at each new level.

Mets vs. Yankees. The value of experience can be clearly seen by looking at the 2000 World Series between the New York Yankees and the New York Mets. The Yankees won, making it 3 World Series wins in a row.

The Yankees had not been playing great baseball towards the end of the regular season. However, they got the hits, made the plays, and came up with good pitching in the playoffs. They were able to elevate their quality of play when it counted.

Meanwhile, the Mets did not play as well as they had during the regular season. They made numerous base-running mistakes and quite often struck out on bad pitches in the dirt. They were too anxious—probably because they had neither the recent playoff nor World Series experience that the Yankees had.

Post season playoffs are an even higher level of play than the regular Major League season, and having more playoff experience proved to be a big advantage for the Yankees.

Experience does not *always* win the World Series, but it always gives you an edge.

16

ATTITUDE AND MENTAL APPROACH

We have talked about the value of concentration, the desire to play, motivation, determination, game situations, experience, and more. *All of these factors help shape our attitude and mental approach to the game.*

Interpersonal Relations

The relations you have with other people are your *interpersonal relations*. In baseball, your interpersonal relations are defined by the way you act and respond to teammates, coaches, managers, parents, officials, and fans.

You should always strive to be enthusiastic and positive—strive to be a good person and respect others.

Being enthusiastic means hustling and showing your love for the game. Being positive means having a can-do attitude, even in the worst situations. Being a good person simply means doing the right thing. Showing respect means being considerate and never insulting.

It is very important that you display these qualities. *In fact, whether you get to play or not can depend directly on your interpersonal relations.* No coach or manager wants to be surrounded by a bunch of rude, negative players. Once you have been labeled a troublemaker or complainer, it can be very hard to shake the negative image. The label will follow you.

If you are trying to make a high school, college, or professional team, imagine that *you* are the manager—*and you have 3 players for only 1 spot*. All 3 players seem to have equal ability. One of these players is always hustling, listens well, and is a joy to be around. The other 2 players are okay guys. Which player will you select?

A player with a good attitude is often taken over a more talented player that management believes will cause problems. Therefore, part of your mental approach to baseball is to always have a good, positive attitude.

Staying on an Even Keel

Staying on an even keel means not getting too excited or too depressed over what happens—it means maintaining your level of composure.

Do not get on that "emotional roller coaster ride." Getting too overjoyed or depressed can be very energy-draining and cause you to play anxiously and unrelaxed.

If you do something great, enjoy it, but act like it is what you are supposed to be able to do. This shows others your confidence and belief in yourself. Along the same lines, do not let mistakes overcome you. Letting your opponents see you frustrated or acting like you have given up gives *them* confidence. Remember that even the best players have bad games.

I will never forget playing against Joe Morgan's AAA Red Sox team in Pawtucket, Rhode Island. It was during a season in the late 1970s, and I was playing for either the Richmond Braves or the Rochester Red Wings (Orioles)—I do not recall which. Morgan's team won virtually every series we played that year—but it was the *way* they won that stays in my memory.

I recall that in most of the games, we would be leading up until the 8th or 9th inning. Then they would get runners on, and Wade Boggs, Sam Bowen, or someone would come through with a double or a home run to beat us. And none of their players who got the hits or scored the runs in the comeback would ever celebrate excessively. This impressed me a great deal. They played as if they were *supposed* to beat us and that really hurt. It got to where many of *us* believed they were supposed to beat us.

The point is, they had the edge on us because they were able to play relaxed and with confidence. Our players would suffer the mental letdown, while they would always have the energy to come back strong again the next night.

Shaping Your Attitude and Mental Approach to Hitting

Shape your attitude and mental approach to hitting by focusing on the following 3 aspects:

1) Self talk
2) Wanting to be the best
3) Concentration level

Self Talk

I would argue that hitting is the most difficult skill to master in all of sports. I say this because of the many fundamentals that must be learned, the precise timing required, the mental aspects involved, the great number of adjustments that must continually be made, and the risk involved. Therefore, your mental approach to hitting must be very special.

The use of "self talk" should be an important part of your mental approach to hitting. Self talk is what you think or say to yourself. When you use positive self talk, you prepare yourself to succeed.

Your self talk should promote confidence, motivation, and concentration. For example, on my walk to the plate I would think or tell myself "I can do it...I can do it." This would give me confidence and relax me. At the plate, I would think "be quick...be quick" if the pitcher had a great fastball, or "wait...wait" if I knew I was going to get a curve. I would remain cool, calm, and collected. Maybe my swing would be great except for overstriding a little. I would think "short stride...short stride." With 2 strikes, I would think "see the ball and hit it."

I am not telling you to go around all day talking to yourself, but use self talk when it helps you play better.

Wanting to be the Best

Hitting ***is*** an attitude. You must *want* to be the best, and only *you* can do that! Between you and the pitcher, you must want to prove you are the better player.

I would not accept letting any pitcher get the best of me. I would know if I was 0-7 against a pitcher, and I would strive to win the next encounter. For motivation, I would make a list of the pitchers I had not done well against. Fortunately, there would not be many on the list at any one time.

I would take extra care in recalling *how* a particular pitcher had gotten me out. When I faced him the next time, I would raise my level of concentration.

Concentration Level

To be the best hitter you can be, you must raise your level of concentration at the plate. This means you put together all the aspects of hitting you have learned—balance, form, desire, motivation, determination—everything. You mentally "lock in" all your swing fundamentals and technique. You are determined to see the ball early and be quick. Your concentration propels you to a higher level!

17

SWITCH-HITTING

Switch-hitting is batting from either side of the plate—right-handed against left-handed pitching and left-handed against right-handed pitching. Being able to switch-hit gives you tremendous advantages. There are 3 great reasons for switch-hitting.

1) To hit for a higher average
2) To avoid injury
3) To stay in the line up

Hitting for a Higher Average

It is easier to hit a ball breaking in to you than one breaking away from you. Switch-hitting places you in this desirable situation every time you go to the plate. The primary reason for this is that your stance and swing are not disturbed by pitches that come *at* you—you do not have to hit those pitches—you only have to avoid them.

When you bat righty vs. righty—or lefty vs. lefty—a big curveball often starts out at you, before breaking down and across the plate.

A good slider can do the same, although pitchers try to throw sliders low and to the outside corner.

As a hitter, your first instinct is to get out of the way of a pitch coming at you. As soon as you have "bailed" away from the plate even a little, you have disrupted your balance and timing. You may also have taken your eye off the ball. If the pitch is a curveball, the result is usually a weak, off-balance swing or a called strike. The end result is a lower batting average.

On the other hand, if you hang in there too long to make sure it is not a breaking ball, you could get hit by a fastball.

Avoiding Injury

Getting hit by a pitch can result in an injury that forces you out of the line up. We all know how dangerous getting "beaned" in the head is, but injuries to ribs, hands, elbows, and other areas can also sideline you—for days, weeks, or even months.

The advantage of switch-hitting is that you can assume any pitch coming at you is a fastball, because the breaking ball starts away from you and breaks in. This makes your decision a quick and easy one—*at* you, "get outta there"—*away* from you, stay in there and hit the ball if it breaks over the plate! *There is no bailing out and having to recover.*

Staying in the Lineup

Avoiding injury is one way of staying in the lineup. Another way switch-hitting keeps you in the lineup is that your manager does not have to "platoon" you, or "pinch-hit" for you. In Little League, these moves are seldom considered. However, in higher levels of baseball, *platooning* and *pinch-hitting* are strategies of the game.

Managers platoon by making their lineups according to who is pitching for the other team. Against right-handed pitchers, they place left-handed batters in the lineup. Against left-handed pitchers, they place right-handed batters in the lineup.

Later in the game, the opposing team may bring in a relief pitcher. If they change from a righty to a lefty—or vice versa—your manager will probably make some pinch-hitting changes. If you bat left-handed and a left-handed pitcher is brought in, you may come out in favor of a right-handed batter—and vice versa.

If you are a switch-hitter, the manager does not have to make these moves with you. *You just turn around and bat the other way!*

Managers make these decisions because they know that the percentages are with them. Most players *do* hit for a higher average when batting left-handed against right-handed pitching—and vice versa. When this trend is broken, it is usually because right-handed hitters go too long without seeing enough left-handed pitching. Historically, there have been more right-handed pitchers than left-handed.

About Switch-Hitters

You may ask why a switch-hitter does not win the batting crown every year. You must realize that there are not that many switch-hitters. Also note that many of baseball's switch-hitters *have* hit for high averages and with power.

Pete Rose, perhaps the greatest hitter of all time, was a switch-hitter. Pete played most of his career with the Cincinnati Reds. Of course, many would argue whether Rose *is* the greatest hitter of all time or not. Pete Rose simply got more hits than anyone else ever has. The best hitters in baseball play for 20 or more years, and only a few ever reach the phenomenal mark of 3,000 hits—Pete Rose had **4,256!**

The greatest *home run* hitter of all time must be Hank Aaron. The Braves slugger belted 755 home runs in his Major League career. Many people still think of Babe Ruth (714 homers) as the greatest home run hitter, because he did so much for the popularity of baseball. Some other notable home run hitters are Willie Mays, who belted 660 homers for the San Francisco Giants, Mark McGwire, and Barry Bonds. Through the 2001 season, McGwire has hit 583 home runs and Bonds 567.

Another great switch-hitter was Yankees center fielder **Mickey Mantle**, who batted cleanup for more championship teams than anyone in history. Mantle hit 536 home runs in his career.

Orioles switch-hitter **Eddie Murray** is remembered as one of the greatest players ever. Eddie got more than 3,000 hits in his career and belted 504 home runs.

Switch-hitting **Chili Davis** retired after the 1999 season with 350 career homers.

Switch-hitter **Reggie Smith** belted 314 home runs and batted over .300 seven times in his career.

Modern-day slugger **Chipper Jones**, switch-hitter for the Atlanta Braves, was named the National League's Most Valuable Player in 1999. Chipper batted .319, with 45 homers and 110 RBI.

Yankees switch-hitter **Bernie Williams** was the American League batting champ in 1999. Bernie hit .342, with 25 homers and 115 RBI.

Can You Switch-hit?

The only way to find out if switch-hitting is for you is to try it. However, you have to put a little time into it. You have to build up your strength and coordination and that does not happen overnight. Your top hand must get strong enough to drive your swing forward and roll over with the same power you have from your strong side.

The idea is to "mirror" what you do from your natural side. However, you may need to make some small adjustments at first. You will not be as quick, because you are not as strong yet. Widen your stance a little and make sure that you hardly stride at all. Do what you learned in the *Swing* chapter to quicken the swing. Take the wrap out of your bat and angle it in the opposite direction if you need to.

Practice for a few months—3 or 4 times a week. At first, just hit soft toss and concentrate on duplicating what you do from your natural side. Work on form and taking a good cut. After a few weeks, start out your practices with a little soft toss and then hit off live pitching.

If you still feel awkward after this period of time, maybe switch-hitting is not for you. On the other hand, if you feel like you are progressing and getting stronger, you may want to stay with it.

Becoming a good switch-hitter requires that you use the keys to success discussed in this book. Another key you can add to the list is **believing**. *You must believe in yourself.* Believing that you can switch-hit will motivate you to practice hard at it.

I was a natural right-handed batter, but I always "messed around" with switch-hitting. However, I never tried it in real games until my second year of professional baseball.

There were a lot of bad, dangerous backgrounds in the Minor Leagues when I played. Trying to pick up the ball out of a gray sky or white sign was too difficult for me, and it was also dangerous. I knew that switch-hitting would give me more time to see the ball before having to make a decision at the plate—and I really believed that I could do it.

My manager was former Major League pitcher, Frank Funk. Fortunately for me, he was a nice enough guy to let me try switch-hitting. At first, I just tried to make contact and beat out a lot of ground balls for hits. I ended up batting .301 and leading the California League in total hits that year.

I gradually got stronger from the left side. Within a few years, I was hitting the ball just as hard from the left side as from the right.

More players could switch-hit if they were encouraged to and if they practiced enough to develop this skill. A great analogy that illustrates this point comes from basketball.

I can clearly remember my aunt taking me to see a high school basketball game when I was just a young boy. It was the 1950s, and we lived in Topeka, Kansas. I remember the players took 2-handed set shots, and they all dribbled with their dominant hand only. Most people back then did not think players could dribble with both hands. Yet, look at today's basketball players. Every player now dribbles with either hand. Although hitting a baseball is more intricate, the principle is the same.

18

GETTING OUT OF THE WAY OF A PITCH

No one likes getting hit by a pitch, but sooner or later everyone does. Sometimes it is unavoidable. Your aim is to avoid serious injury. Getting out of the way of a pitch quickly and safely is a major concern for every ballplayer.

When getting out of the way of a pitch, you should focus on 2 goals:

1) Protect your vital areas.
2) Lessen the force of impact.

How to Protect Vital Areas

You can use technique to better protect the face, head, ribs, hands, and elbows, as well as most of the body. Use the specific technique designed for the area of the body you are protecting.

A pitch thrown at the head. This pitch is known as the "beanball." If you are batting and a fastball is coming in straight at your head, you must get down in a hurry. You may have to throw your feet up and "hit the dirt" to do so, and you must turn your face *away from the pitcher.* At the same time, try to move away from the pitch (towards the backstop).

A pitch thrown anywhere from the shoulder to the waist. When avoiding this "up and in" pitch, turn your face away from the pitcher as before. Pull your front elbow and hands in and behind the body (fig. 41). Body movement should be away from the pitch.

Avoiding the pitch thrown up and in.
fig. 41

A pitch thrown from the waist to the knees. Turn and move away from the pitch—or, jump out of the way if there is time.

A pitch thrown lower than the knees. Either jump over this pitch if it is low enough or slide-jump away from the plate to avoid it.

Lessen the Force of Impact

Lessening the force of impact means not getting hit as hard. If you are moving away from a ball that hits you, you will sustain less injury than if you were standing still or moving forward. This is why moving away from the pitch is emphasized as a means of protecting your vital areas.

A great example of this is to consider 2 cars in a crash. If a car traveling 40 mph hits a car going 20 mph in the same direction, the force of impact is 20 mph. However, if the 2 cars crash while heading into each other, the force of impact is 60 mph. Moving away from an object lessens impact, but moving towards it increases impact.

As a practice drill, I pitched tennis balls to my son when he was 10 years old. The pitch could either be at him or over the plate. When the pitch came at him, he would have to follow the correct technique for getting out of the way of each specific pitch. When the pitch came over the plate, he had to be able to take a good cut at the ball without having bailed out.

Why *practice* this? It is better to be hit by a few tennis balls in practice than to get hit in a game and sustain a serious injury. Remember that baseball is a game of repetition—and safe play should be automatic!

19

BUNTING

I never enjoyed bunting because I had a deep desire to hit the ball hard every time I batted. However, bunting is a necessary part of baseball. It helps the team win games—and it can also help you.

There are 3 reasons to bunt:

1) To move base runners up a base
2) To get a hit
3) To improve your batting average by forcing the defense to play in

Bunting to Move Runners up a Base. This is called "sacrifice" bunting. With no outs or 1 out, you sacrifice bunt a runner from first to second so he can score on a base hit. With no outs, you sacrifice bunt a runner from second to third because there are many ways to score from third base with 1 out—a hit, a fly ball, a ground ball, an error, a wild pitch, a passed ball, a balk, a bases-loaded walk, or a "squeeze play."

Bunting for a Hit. When infielders play you deep, bunting for a hit can be highly successful. Fielders do not have enough time to run way in, field the ball, and throw you out. You get the hit.

Forcing the Defense to Play in. *If infielders know you will bunt, they have to play you in.* When they do, you are able to drive more balls past them for hits—and more hits means a higher average.

For *many* years, the standard method of sacrifice bunting was to stand facing the pitcher with your top hand "choked up" on the bat (fig. 42).

Standard bunting stance.
fig. 42

I have always considered this stance foolish and dangerous. It is very hard to avoid a pitch thrown at you when you are in this position.

It has always made more sense to me to simply turn the shoulders and pivot the back foot a little (fig. 43). There is nothing you can do using the standard method that you cannot do using the safer **"turn and pivot"** method.

When I played in the 1970s, every professional baseball organization used the standard bunting stance to move runners up. Fortunately for me, my managers always allowed me to bunt my way as long as I did the job. Today, it appears that every organization is using (or will soon be using) the *turn and pivot* method—it has become the new standard.

"Turn and pivot" bunting stance.
fig. 43

Where to Sacrifice Bunt

If you are bunting a runner from first base to second, bunt the ball down the first base side—the third baseman and pitcher have an easier play to second.

When bunting a runner from second base to third, bunt down the third base side—make the third baseman leave the base open and make the play.

If you are bunting a runner from third base to home on the "squeeze play," just make sure you get the bunt down. A pop-up usually results in a double play.

Where to Bunt for a Hit

The 2 best places to bunt for a hit are down the third base line and at the second baseman.

When a right-handed batter bunts for a hit down the third base line, or a left-handed batter to the right side of the field, it is called "drag bunting." Bunting for a hit to the opposite field is called "push bunting."

When bunting down the third base line, your goal is to place your bunt as close to the line as possible. If you miss placing it close to the line, make sure you miss foul. You do not want the pitcher throwing you out. Close to the line also makes the third baseman's throw a longer and tougher one.

When bunting at the second baseman, you must bunt the ball straight at the second base position and hard enough to get it past the pitcher. Force the second baseman to field it. Bunting too close to first base allows the first baseman to field the ball and throw to the pitcher, who is covering first.

How to Bunt for a Hit

Right-handed Batters. When drag bunting down the third base line, first disguise your bunt. Let your stance and body language make it look like you want to swing away. Wait as long as possible before making your move. Then pull the hands and bat downward and forward a little in a chopping motion, as you step away from the plate with your right foot (fig. 44).

Contact point for right-handed drag bunt.
fig. 44

Time your bunt so that at the moment you are contacting the ball, you are also planting and pushing yourself forward with the right foot. This gives you a quick start out of the box. Your first step out is with your right foot.

When pushing your bunt at the second baseman, follow the same technique, only push the bat forward more and hit the ball a little harder.

Left-handed batters. To drag bunt at the second baseman, disguise your bunt and wait as long as possible. Take a short stride for deception as you move forward with the body. Make contact and take off. Your first step out is with the left foot (fig. 45).

Contact point for left-handed drag bunt.
fig. 45

When pushing your bunt down the third base line, follow the same technique, only make contact near the end of the bat to "deaden" your bunt.

Whether sacrificing, push bunting, or drag bunting, *always try to keep the bat out front with the hitting end up slightly* (figs. 42-45).

20

CHECKLIST

Let's make a checklist of the major points to focus on when going to bat. List these major points on an index card and review them from time to time. Numbers 1-9 set you up for your swing. Numbers 10-20 fall within your swing.

SETUP

1) Select the right bat.

2) Stand in the back of the box.

3) Set your feet right.

4) Get the right grip.

5) Cock your wrists.

6) Balance your weight properly (60%-40%).

7) Place your hands in the hitting position.

8) Position your elbows, shoulders, and bat correctly.

9) Do not get "frozen" at the plate.

SWING

10) Take a short stride.

11) Bring your head in as the body turns out.

12) Point your front foot out slightly when striding.

13) Turn your back foot in when striding.

14) Shift your weight forward *a little* when swinging.

15) Concentrate on timing.

16) Use the 6 degree swing angle.

17) Extend your arms when you can.

18) Hit the ball out in front when you can.

19) Snap your wrists.

20) Follow through.

Remember the keys that lead to hitting success—such as natural ability, love, desire, motivation, determination, practice and hard work, experience, staying on an even keel, shaping your attitude and mental approach, and believing in yourself.

Note: Some of the players' statistics in this book were obtained from CNN/SI.

AFTERWORD

Whether perfecting or correcting your hitting technique, it is helpful to have a capable person observe and evaluate your actions. Sometimes you cannot see, feel, or even detect what you are doing wrong. Many former professional players are now available for hitting instruction. Just make sure you get a good one.

The best way to hit is the way you hit best. If you get in a hitting slump, go back to doing what you were doing when you were hitting the ball well. Slumps are usually caused by changes in your hitting technique that you do not realize you have made.

When you go to bat: prepare for the pitch as you like—place your hands in the hitting position just before it is time to swing—and use the *quickest swing*. (It is okay to wrap and hitch *if it works for you*.)

You can follow the fundamentals I have given you and still create a *style* of your own. Slight changes in stance, preparation, and technique are okay, as long as you still get good results.

If your manager or coach tells you not to use what you have learned in this book, try to get on another team.

Coaches and parents: Be patient. *Fundamentals that seem simple can actually be difficult to carry out*, especially for kids 12 and under. With *very* young kids, just the weight of the bat can prevent assuming a good stance or taking a good swing. So don't get mad. Give the kids time and understanding.

I *will not* wish you luck, because I do not believe in luck. *Use the hitting fundamentals, the keys to success, and the mental aspects you have just learned to be the best baseball hitter you can be!*

Author's Baseball Career

Professional Career

1972	A Giants	Decater, IL
1973	A Giants	Fresno, CA—led league in hits and at-bats, hit .301.
1974	AA Giants	Amarillo, TX—hit .296
	AAA Giants	Phoenix, AZ—hit .313
1975	AAA Giants	Phoenix, AZ—led league in triples, batted .320 (third in the league).
1976	AAA Giants	Phoenix, AZ—batted .325
	AAA Braves	Richmond, VA—batted .304
	N.L. Braves	Atlanta, GA
1977	AAA Braves	Richmond, VA—batted .314
1978	A.L. White Sox	Chicago, IL
	AAA White Sox	Des Moines, IA
1979	AAA Orioles	Rochester, NY
1980	AAA Orioles	Rochester, NY—player/coach for Doc Edwards

Professional Winter Baseball

1972	Arizona Instructional League	Phoenix, AZ
1973	Arizona Instructional League	Phoenix, AZ

1973 Guaymas, Mexico—began playing winter ball in the *Mexican Pacific Winter League* (comprised of Mexico's best, United States' prospects, and Major Leaguers)

1974 Guaymas, Mexico

1975 Guaymas, Mexico

1976 Guaymas, Mexico—batted .328 (second in league), second in home runs (in the league), picked up by Hermosillo, Mexico for playoffs—won league, placed second in Carribean World Series in San Juan, Puerto Rico.

1977 Guaymas, Mexico—player/manager, picked up by Obregon, Mexico for playoffs.

1978 Obregon, Mexico—manager

Amateur (starting with high school)

A. School

1965 Chamberlain High School—Tampa, FL

1966 Chamberlain High School—Tampa, FL
all-Western Conference shortstop

1969 Brevard Junior College—Cocoa, FL

1970 Brevard Junior College—Cocoa, FL
Honorable Mention all-District

1971 Southern Illinois University—Carbondale, IL
batted .378, all-Conference, all-World Series (batted .450)

1972 Southern Illinois University—Carbondale, IL
batted .412, all-Conference

B. Summer Leagues

1968 Detroit Free Press League—Detroit, MI
batting champ in national tournament, hit .625.

1969 Cape Cod League—Orleans, MA

1970 Cape Cod League—Orleans, MA
batting champ, hit .378

1971 Basin League—Winner, SD

Post Professional Career

1982-2002	20 years of coaching youth sports and working with children
1996	Forest Hills Pony Baseball—managed Pinto winter maroon team.
1997	Forest Hills Pony Baseball—managed Mustang winter Dodgers.
1998	Northside Little League—managed winter A's.
2000	Forest Hills Pony Baseball—managed winter Cardinals.
2001	Forest Hills Pony Baseball—managed Bronco A's, managed Pony winter A's.